The Cathedral of San Rufino in Assisi. Here Francis, Clare, and all the first Franciscans from Assisi were baptized.

The impressive medieval castle, Rocca Maggiore, dominates Assisi from its steep hilltop position on Mount Subasio. It reminds visitors of the city's past conflicts, as it represents the feudal power structure.

The Chiesa Nuova (New Church) is built over the site believed to be the home and shop of Pietro di Bernardone.

San Damiano is a lovely sanctuary about one mile outside the city walls. This is the first church Francis rebuilt.

In Francis' era, there were several leper hospitals in the valley below Assisi. This church, Santa Maria Maddalena, served the lepers who were banished there.

The crucifix that spoke to Francis, telling him, "Go and rebuild my house, which has fallen into ruin."

The Basilica of Santa Maria degli Angeli houses the Portiuncula.

The Portiuncula (*Porziuncola* in Italian) was Francis' favorite church. Here he died on the night of October 3, 1226.

Francis and the first friars lived simply in two huts near Rivotorto (meaning "crooked stream").

The lovely Carceri hermitage above Assisi is located within a crevice on Mount Subasio.

The mountain hermitage in Tuscany where Francis received the stigmata in 1224.

The ornate, two-tier basilica built over the tomb of Francis.

Panorama of Assisi.

A statue of Francis in front of St. John Lateran in Rome. Francis is depicted preventing the façade from crumbling, commemorating the dream of Pope Innocent III in 1209.

St. Francis of Assisi

PASSION, POVERTY, AND THE MAN WHO TRANSFORMED THE CATHOLIC CHURCH

SECOND EDITION

St. Francis of Assisi

PASSION, POVERTY, AND THE MAN WHO TRANSFORMED THE CATHOLIC CHURCH

SECOND EDITION

BRET THOMAN, O.F.S.

WITH A FOREWORD BY
FATHER MURRAY BODO, O.F.M.

TAN Books
Charlotte, North Carolina

Cover illustration: *The Dream of Innocent III*, 1297-99 (fresco), Giotto di Bondone (c.1266-1337) / San Francesco, Upper Church, Assisi, Italy / Bridgeman Images

Cover design by David Ferris Design

ISBN: 978-1-61890-770-7

Published in the United States by
TAN Books
P.O. Box 410487
Charlotte, NC 28241
www.TANBooks.com

Printed and bound in the United States of America

CONTENTS

This book is dedicated to my son, Iacopo . . .

May you keep this book with you throughout your life's journey. May the spirit and intercession of St. Francis guide you, inspire you, move you, and make you enthusiastic in all you do.

Thank you for giving me the gift and joy of fatherhood.

FOREWORD

Father Murray Bodo, O.F.M.

SIX years before he died, St. Francis said to his brothers gathered at the Chapter of Mats of 1220, "The
Lord told me that he wanted to make a new fool of me in
the world, and God does not want to lead us by any other
knowledge than that." He was responding to pressure from
some learned brothers who were changing the direction of
the Order by building houses of study that were not in con-
formity to the poor dwellings the brothers were supposed to
dwell in. He saw learning as an ominous new direction that
could separate the brothers from Gospel poverty and from
the spirit of prayer and holy devotion.

How Francis came to found an Order based on radical
Gospel poverty and how that option for poverty helped
restore the medieval Church is beautifully drawn in these
pages. Bret Thoman writes with Franciscan simplicity and
clarity a Life of St. Francis that, although it is based on
extensive sources both medieval and modern, reads like a
novel. The point of view is from within the characters who
people the world of Francis of Assisi, but especially from
within the consciousness of Francis himself.

And like a novel it tells the story well, making of Francis
a paradigm of the quintessential Gospel person. It is a story
that begins in earnest as a story of the medieval Church

itself when Francis hears the Gospel read on the Feast of St. Matthias on February 24, 1208. It was then that he finally knew what the shape and content of his and the brothers' lives would be.

At first when he heard Christ say from the San Damiano Cross, "Francis, go and repair my house which, as you see, is falling into ruins," he took Christ's words literally and began to rebuild the small church of San Damiano outside the walls of Assisi. But once other brothers began to join him, he began to wonder how they were to live together. And then he heard the Gospel on that fateful day in 1208 when Jesus said that his true disciples should "take no gold, or silver, or copper in their belts, no bag for their journey, or sandals or a staff" (Mt 10:9–10).

Francis was filled with joy and cried out, "This is what I want; this is what I desire with all my heart!" And that is how he began to understand what kind of "new fools" he and his brothers were to become. He would take these words of Christ and other similar sayings to the pope and ask for his approval.

Thoman then tells the story of Francis and the brothers going to Rome a year later, in 1209, carrying with them only a collection of Gospel passages, now lost to history, to seek papal approval of the life and rule of the poor lesser brothers of Assisi. At one point in his dialogue with Pope Innocent III, Thoman has Francis say to the pope,

> I am called to the *Vita Evangelica*, the Gospel life of total poverty. . . . Together with my first brothers, Scripture showed us to give away everything we had: "If you would be perfect, go, sell what you possess and give to the poor, and you will have treasure in heaven; and come, follow me" (Mt 19:21);

"Take nothing for your journey" (Lk 9:3); and "If any man would come after me, let him deny himself and take up his cross daily and follow me" (Lk 9:23). This is what we have sought to do. This is how we wish to live–according to the words of Jesus Christ himself.

This embrace of the total poverty of the Gospel is what made Francis and his brothers something new. Pope Innocent verbally approved this tentative rule; and what we know today as the Franciscan Order began, a group of brothers who, in the words of their final Rule, approved by Pope Honorius III in 1223, vowed to live *without anything of their own.*

The drama and the romance, the joy and suffering of those beginnings and of the man who was the instrument of that Gospel revolution, is the story *St. Francis of Assisi: Passion, Poverty and the Man Who Transformed the Catholic Church.* Thoman tells that story masterfully, and in the telling not only reveals his gifts as a story-teller but opens to us the heart of the man whose story he is telling. In the process, he also tells the story of the Franciscans' relationship to the Church at the beginning of the thirteenth century. Through multiple footnotes, he also authenticates the details of a story that is part history and part imagined. This combination of fact and imagination make, in Thoman's hand, a beautiful and believable story of a passion and poverty that gave the world a new kind of fool.

FATHER MURRAY BODO, O.F.M.

PREFACE

IT was 1992 and I was a young college student in Florence learning Italian. As an antidote to the drudgery of subjunctive moods and irregular pluperfect tenses, our school organized weekend excursions to nearby cities and places of interest. One Saturday we went to Assisi.

As our chartered tour bus rambled southeast along Italy's A1 autostrada, I recall being taken by Italy's breathtaking landscape. My first time outside the United States, I marveled as Tuscany's gentle rolling hills morphed into Umbria's harsher Apennine peaks. And all the while I was blissfully unaware as to what lay in store for me.

When we arrived in Assisi, I looked up at the medieval town built many centuries ago of stone carved out of nearby Mount Subasio and immediately sensed something unusual about the place: I felt it was holy. This was a strange sensation for me, for I had been long absent from any church . . . and Christian way of life. Though I had been baptized in a Protestant church and had believed in God as a child, youthful pride had then gotten the better of me and I was in open rebellion against all that smacked of "organized religion."

Our day began with a visit through the storied thirteenth-century majestic basilica which conserved the remains of Assisi's most famous son. As I wondered at the Romanesque-Gothic architecture and the still extraordinarily vibrant artwork despite the ravages of almost eight centuries, I was struck all the more by the stories narrated pictorially by Giotto in his celebrated frescoes. Given my Protestant upbringing, I was embarrassingly ignorant of the lives of the saints. And this was the first time I had ever heard the name St. Francis of Assisi.

As our faithful Italian professor tactfully broke open the legends, I had honestly never heard of anyone doing such a thing so radical, so drastic, for nothing other than love of God. But as I discovered more about this gentle Umbrian saint, I began to feel unsettled, as there was something uncomfortably familiar about his life trajectory. As I learned about Francis' bourgeois background as the son of a wealthy merchant, I considered how I had grown up as the son of an airline captain in an affluent American suburb. While the young Francis sought to improve his lot through knighthood, I was likewise concerned with little other than myself—my career decisions and my wants. Yet after an encounter with the Crucified Christ, Francis was so infused by the love of God that he gave away everything he possessed. And it was there that any similarities ended, as I had not yet had my encounter with the God of mercy and forgiveness.

At the conclusion of the tour, we had some free time. While other students poked around the souvenir stands near the parking lot, I wanted more. So I set out toward the center of town to explore. While I was enthralled by Assisi's characteristic medieval walls and stone facades, I happened to notice an elderly woman slip through a glass door off the main street. Beyond was a chapel and more frescoes. Whether out of curiosity or the prompting of the Spirit, I followed her in.

Immediately I was struck at how this chapel, though also beautifully decorated, was markedly different from the bustling basilica just a few steps away. Instead of the hubbub of tourists and pilgrims, there were only two or three people, including a veiled nun, and all were praying silently. Though it felt unnatural, I did what the others were doing: I, too, knelt down in prayer. And as I closed my eyes, something began to stir. I had known it once as a child, but it had long since been dormant.

I recalled moments from those few short years in Sunday School as a child when I had experienced the presence of God in my heart. I remembered innocence, the desire to please God and be a good person. I pondered how I had once promised I would never do bad things, as well as the guilt I felt after disobeying my parents or telling a white lie.

Suddenly so many things I was clinging to at that point in my life seemed unimportant, even silly. I clearly saw that my attitude toward religion was shallow and self-centered and that God was infinitely greater than the box in which I had pridefully enclosed him. I recalled the first few recently memorized lines of Dante's "Divine Comedy": *"Nel mezzo del cammin' di nostra vita, mi ritrovai per una selva oscura che la diritta via era smarrita"* ("In the middle of our life's journey, I found myself in a dark forest, as the straight way had been lost.")

In that moment, despite my unworthiness, I was illuminated with enough light to clearly discern the "dark forest" about me, that I had lost the "straight path." Yet something within also told me that I would soon be led on the "straight way." There, in the stillness of that quiet little chapel, a sense of hope flooded from somewhere deep within. And though I had no idea where I would be headed, I knew it would be to a better place.

At the end of the summer, I returned home with a decent command of the Italian language but, more importantly, the experience of Saint Francis of Assisi impressed on my heart. And three years later—when I was ready—I made my journey into the Catholic Church. It was only natural for me to choose St. Francis of Assisi as my confirmation name.

I soon returned to Florence to complete a master's degree in Italian. And it was then when my path would cross with Katia. Originally from southern Italy, she had relocated to Assisi for the purpose of attending university; instead, she, too, ended up smitten by the seraphic saint. Through the example and direction of Assisi's many friars and nuns, her childhood Catholic faith came alive, and she felt the fullness of God's love for her in Scripture that spoke to her saying, "you shall be called 'My Delight is in her,' and your land 'Espoused'" (Is 62:4 NABRE).

After Katia and I married and made our home in the United States, we both wanted to continue our Franciscan journey, and so we entered the Secular Franciscan Order. Given our experiences, we had a desire to share with others what we had received in Assisi. Thus, we began organizing and accompanying English-speaking groups to Assisi and to the Rieti Valley, Laverna, the Marches, and Rome.

We were delighted to discover that most receive the seraphic city as we had—not as tourists who are largely untouched by Italy's innumerable monuments and ruins as they snap photos and sample gelatos in Rome, Florence, and Venice. Instead, they are pilgrims. They instinctively know that their journey to Assisi is as that of so many who have been before: friars and sisters, laypersons and priests, wayfarers and travelers, painters and poets, people from every nation and race. Assisi for these people is an encounter with ancient stones, living stones, that still sing of the life of Francis.

As they tread in Francis' footsteps along those same cobblestone paths, their spirit is drawn upward, in transcendence, toward Mount Subasio where Francis once gazed up at almighty God. Yet the journey also requires that they go down, immanently, to the plains of the Spoleto Valley below where Francis renounced his privileged worldly status and lowered himself at the feet of the leper. And in this, are they not walking in much larger footsteps? Are they not following the One whom "the highest heavens cannot contain" (1 Kgs 8:27 NABRE)? Who "emptied himself, taking the form of a slave, coming in human likeness" (Phil 2:6–7 NABRE)? Who "became poor, . . . so that by his poverty you might become rich" (2 Cor 8:9 NABRE)? It is in this journey, following these footsteps, in which something happens and they are transformed.

When one has an encounter with the love of God, a transformative enduring encounter, there is a natural tendency to "go out." What God gave Saint Francis, he could not contain within himself and it flowed to others. In a cycle of receiving and giving, that grace has been received and given now for over eight centuries. This book is the fruit of what I have received and now give.

In this second edition of *St. Francis of Assisi: Passion, Poverty, and the Man Who Transformed the Catholic Church*, I changed very little from the first edition. This book is not a critical biography or a theological treatise. Though there is a Franciscan intellectual tradition going back to the early *Vitae* of St. Bonaventure and Thomas of Celano, this book, instead, draws on the popular story-telling tradition of the early friars—the tales, short-stories, and the eye-witness accounts. It follows in the line of the "Legend of the Three Companions" or the "Little Flowers" which, in unpretentious and straightforward language, sought to portray the essence of the "fool for Christ"—the man whose life embodied the message of St. Paul, who wrote: "For the foolishness of God is wiser than human wisdom, and the weakness of God is stronger than human strength" (1 Cor 1:25 NABRE).

Though there are many books about Francis, they are each unique and vary largely according to (the biases of) the author. As already highlighted, this book is the work of someone who is a convert to Catholicism thanks largely to the story of St. Francis of Assisi, a professed member of the Secular Franciscan Order (once known as Third Order of St. Francis), a teacher of Franciscan spirituality and formation minister in his fraternity, a former faculty member at St. Francis University's ICFL program, and a pilgrimage guide. While not intending to be a form of contemporary "hagiography," it does strive to bring the reader back in time to the places one can visit as if on pilgrimage as well as into the spirit of St. Francis in order to, hopefully, inspire a change of heart in the reader and promote the life of St. Francis.

Every time I have walked the streets of Assisi with others, I am taken back to my first encounter I had there. And it is my hope that the readers of this book receive that same gift of inner joy and singular peace that comes from God and was experienced by St. Francis.

"PAX ET BONUM" (PEACE AND GOOD).

Bret Thoman, OFS

ACKNOWLEDGMENTS

IT is said that a book is written not by a person, but by a community. That is certainly the case with this book.

Thanks to Regis Armstrong, O.F.M. Cap., whose translations of the writings of St. Francis and the sources were foundational for this book: *Excerpts from Francis and Clare: The Complete Works* (Paulist Press) and *Francis of Assisi: Early Documents* (New City Press) in three volumes, *The Saint* (1999), *The Founder* (2001), and *The Prophet* (2001). These texts are, without a doubt, essential for getting to know the historical Francis.

My favorite modern biography about St. Francis was written by the veritable Renaissance man Arnaldo Fortini. A native of Assisi, he was an historian, poet, attorney, and mayor of Assisi before and during World War II. Fortini did monumental research on the life of Francis leading to his masterpiece, *Francis of Assisi*, translated by Helen Moak (out of print, but accessible online). The fact that Fortini and Francis were both "sons of Assisi" and his access to the Assisi archives gave him unparalleled insight into the life and person of Francis.

Thanks to Father Raniero Cantalamessa, O.F.M. Cap.; Sister Ilia Delio, O.S.F.; Father Martin Breski, O.F.M. Conv.; Tibor Kauser, O.F.S.; Jerry Rousseau, O.F.S.; Father Albert Haase, O.F.M.; Father Murray Bodo, O.F.M.; Doug Clorey, O.F.S.; Father Angelo Ison, O.F.M.; and Madeline

Nugent, C.F.P., for taking the time to read my book and offer heartfelt endorsements.

Thank you also Bishop Gregory J. Hartmayer, O.F.M. Conv., of Savannah for your invaluable time spent in reading my book and writing a nice foreword. Thanks are also due to Nicole Barresi for assisting as a reader.

I would like especially to mention my eternal gratitude to the late Father Linus DeSantis, O.F.M. Conv. (1943–2015), not only for your "labor of love" as reader and editor for this book but also for being my spiritual director and pilgrimage guide for so many years. Thank you for all you did for us, and please continue guiding us and looking after us!

Finally, I would like to thank the O.F.M. friars, the Alcantarine Sisters, and the Poor Clare sisters of the Marches Province in Italy—especially Father Ferdinando Campana, O.F.M. (current provincial minister), Sister Armanda Parenti, and Mother Chiara Laura Serboli, O.S.C. (abbess of the monastery of Camerino). Without their initiatives and support, we would never have been able to accomplish what we have done in Italy. More than anyone else, the Italian friars and Poor Clares have taught us what it means to be Franciscan.

Most of all, I would like to thank my family and my wife, Katia, for supporting and loving me in all my endeavors!

1

NATIVITY

*And while they were there, the time came for her to be deliv-
ered. And she gave birth to her first-born son and wrapped
him in swaddling cloths, and laid him in a manger, because
there was no place for them in the inn.*

LUKE 2:6–7

P ICA was nearing the end of her term. Her friends
and the women of the neighborhood tended to her
in her home joyfully as they all looked forward to the
birth of her first child. Her husband, Pietro, was away in
France on business. Yet when the expected day arrived
and passed, the women became anxious and began to fear
for Pica's health.

Then a strange pilgrim came to the door of her house
with a mysterious message for the young expectant mother
from Provençal, France: she would be able to give birth
only in a stable.[1] So Pica was taken to the family horse

---

1 Today, a church known as the Chiesa Nuova (New Church) is built
over the site believed to be the birth home of St. Francis. Located just
off the Piazza del Commune, the church was constructed in 1615 by the
king of Spain, and is still the most recently built church within the ancient
city walls—hence its name. A tradition dating from the thirteenth century

stable next to the house where, among an ox and a donkey, she immediately gave birth to a son.[2]

When Pica, a pious and gentle woman, looked at her son, she immediately knew what to name him. A child's name in that era was very important, as a name would influence one's entire life. Pica was attuned to the ways of God and she knew in her heart that her son would do great things for God.

She would name her firstborn son after the Baptist—an ascetic and herald of the messiah. As if a prophecy, she gave him the name John, which means "God is gracious."[3] Pica took her son to the cathedral of Assisi near the remains

---

placed this site as the home and shop of Pietro di Bernardone, although there is little historical evidence to support it.

In the rear of the church is a cell commemorating Francis' brief imprisonment by his father. To the left of the main altar is an exit leading to the street level below, where the family shop would have been. Regardless of the authenticity of this tradition, we can imagine Francis playing here as a child and later carousing through the streets with his friends. After his conversion, we can envision Francis begging for stones, singing praises to God, and blessing the townspeople here.

2 About fifty yards away from the New Church, down an alley alongside the church, is a chapel known as San Francesco Piccolino. According to tradition (also dating from the thirteenth century), this was formerly an animal stall where Francis was born. A Latin inscription above the archway reads: "This oratory [chapel] was a stable of ox and donkey, where St. Francis, wonder of the world, was born." Today people come here to pray for their children and healthy pregnancies.

3 The original sources refer to Francis' baptismal name as Giovanni (John). See Thomas of Celano, "The Remembrance of the Desire of a Soul," in *Francis of Assisi: Early Documents*, ed. and trans. Regis J. Armstrong, vol. 2, *The Founder* (Hyde Park, NY: New City Press, 2000), chap. 1, 3; and "The Legend of the Three Companions," in *Francis of Assisi: Early Documents*, vol. 2, *The Founder*, chap. 1, 2. All the early sources refer to Pica, Francis' mother, as being a pious woman.

of Assisi's patron saint, San Rufino, and had him baptized there at the baptistery.[4] Francis would be baptized within a particular local church in the line of great saints.[5]

However, when Pica's husband came back from France, he refused to call his son after a desert preacher-hermit who dressed in a tunic, drank from streams, and ate locusts and wild honey (see Mt 3:4). Pietro was religious, but he was accustomed more to the ways of the world than to the ways of God. He declared, instead, that his firstborn son would be named Francis after his favorite country, France.[6]

In this way, his son's name would pay homage to the great country where he had made his fortune buying extravagant clothes and garments. His son would not bear the name of a poor penitent; instead, he would be named in honor of wealth, grandiosity, and commerce. His father,

---

4 The actual baptistery in which Francis was baptized is currently in the cathedral of San Rufino in Assisi, although it may have been in the former cathedral, St. Mary Major, in Francis' era. What is known about St. Rufinus comes from the apocryphal legends. It appears that he was a bishop from Asia Minor who came to Italy in the fourth century to preach and evangelize. The local pagan authorities resisted, he was beaten, weights were chained to his neck, and he was thrown into the Chiascio River in Costano five miles southwest of Assisi. His remains were recovered by local Christians and entombed in a chapel near Costano until the eleventh century. Then they were brought inside the city walls of Assisi and placed in the present church, which was completely rebuilt in the twelfth century.

5 It may seem somewhat ironic that St. Francis is the patron saint of the country of Italy, while the patron saint of his birth town, Assisi, is still St. Rufinus, as he was in the time of Francis himself.

6 The Italian name given by his father was Francesco. His given name at that time was less a proper name and more an adjective for the country, France. A more accurate translation of the name would be "French-ish" or "Frenchy." In all actuality, his name, Francis, was more a nickname than an actual name. His real name remained his baptismal name, John.

too, believed that his son would do great things; however, his son would be a worldly prince, not a spiritual one.

Francis indeed grew up intelligent and was given numerous natural talents and gifts. Yet his character was proud and he was known to be self-serving. He was crowned "Lord of the Merrymakers" and he often caroused about the city of Assisi reveling and singing with his boisterous companions late into the night without a care in the world.

Francis often presided over great festivals and banquets for his friends, offering everyone fine foods and wines, sensual perfumes, magnificent clothes, expensive decorations, charming music, and dancing. He was a spendthrift, always buying and dressing in the best clothes.[7] Sometimes his father remonstrated with his son for his extravagant ways and the townspeople criticized him for spending more than his social position should have permitted.

Francis followed his father in his business profession as a merchant. However, he was more good-natured and generous with others, unlike his father, who was known to be miserly. In fact, Francis believed that his family had more than enough, which is why he was always giving wealth away with an open hand to the poor who asked.[8]

---

7 "Francis was intent on games and songs; and day and night he roamed about the city of Assisi." "Three Companions," chap. 1, 2. Before his conversion, he is described as "lavish, vain, worldly, proud, a spendthrift."

8 See "Three Companions," chap. 1, 2. Cf. "Even as a young man Francis had an openhanded sympathy for the poor which God had inspired in his heart." Bonaventure of Bagnoregio, "The Major Legend of Saint Francis," in *Francis of Assisi: Early Documents*, ed. and trans. Regis J. Armstrong, vol. 2, *The Founder* (Hyde Park, NY: New City Press, 2000), chap. 1, 1.

He was often magnanimous, courteous, generous, and elegant. In fact, at times, the townspeople recognized his greatness of spirit and good manners. Indeed, young Francis' popularity spread throughout the city so much that everyone who knew him believed that he would one day be something great—like a prince.

His mother, however, knew in her heart that he was destined to greatness of spirit. She said, as another prophecy, "What do you think this son of mine shall become? You will see that he shall merit to become a son of God."[9]

One day, it happened that a poor man was going through the streets of Assisi begging when he came upon Francis. Beggars were everywhere then, as it did not take much to become poor. It only took a serious fall or injury, disease, one's shop burning down, or a bad harvest. As soon as this man saw Francis, he spread his garment on the ground before him and exclaimed to all who were within earshot, "Francis is worthy of reverence and he is destined to do great things in the near future. He will be magnificently honored by all!"[10]

Francis was not yet attuned to the ways of God, and he did not understand the meaning of this poor man's prophecy. He had been told his entire life that he would do great things. Francis believed this prophecy was a fulfillment of his childhood dream—to become a knight.

---

9 See Celano, "Remembrance," chap. 1, 3; and "Three Companions," chap. 1, 2–3.

10 This prophecy is only recorded in Bonaventure, "Major Legend," chap. 1, 1. It is not in the other early sources. Giotto included the scene in his cycle of frescoes in the Upper Basilica of St. Francis in Assisi.

2

WAR

*They shall beat their swords into plowshares, and their
spears into pruning hooks.*

ISAIAH 2:4

IT was November 1202. The sun was just rising behind
Mount Subasio in the east.[1] Francis—Assisi's most
promising citizen—was already awake before the bells
rang. He had hardly slept, so great was his excitement.

The drums of war were beating, and Assisi was at it
again with neighboring Perugia. The twenty-year-old son
of Pietro di Bernardone heard that drumbeat, too, and was
thrilled to be part of it. That day he would take up arms and
fight in the Assisian army against Perugia, prove his valor
on the battlefield, and become a knight!

Francis got out of bed and splashed water quietly on
his arms and face as he tried not to wake his younger
brother, Angelo. He looked out the narrow window of his
bedroom in his father's middle-class home and gazed up
the hill toward the Cathedral of San Rufino. He could see

---

1 Mount Subasio, on the western edge of the Apennine mountain range,
stands at just over 4,200 feet sea level. Assisi is on its northwestern slope.

some of the great tower-like houses of the nobility still standing.

Known as the *Majores* (Majors) of Assisi, they lived up the slopes of Mount Subasio in upper Assisi. Most of their fortresses had been razed to the ground four years earlier during Assisi's civil war when the *Minores* rose up against them. Francis had taken part in that battle, as well, when his father and brother—and the other middle-class merchant families known as the Minors—fought against them.

Francis had been looking up in that direction his entire life, dreaming of becoming a knight. Since the civil war, most of the knights were gone now. But as a boy, they had always fired Francis' imagination with their proud coat of arms ostentatiously displaying their family heritage over the heavy, wooden doors. He had been impressed by the noblemen and knights decked out in their fine leather gloves, boots, cloaks, colorful hose, and swords. As they moved through the streets, people got out of their way.

He had observed the extraordinarily beautiful noble women who were always dressed in fine gowns and jewels. None of the nobility lifted a hand in their houses or fields; their servants and beasts did all the manual labor. Today it would finally happen. He was going to become one of them—a great prince!

As Francis descended the stairs, he glanced through the window on the opposite side of the house down toward the valley. In the distance, he could see the peasants hard at work in the fields. Francis' grandfather, Bernardone, had been born a peasant and worked in one of those same fields in his youth. He was fortunate to have gotten away from the backbreaking misery and poverty of the fields after he began accompanying an uncle on cloth-buying business trips to the north that were then beginning to boom.

When Francis' father, Pietro, grew up, he helped his father develop a very successful family business specializing in textiles.[2] The Bernardone household now stood in the middle of Assisi, near the marketplace, where all the merchants lived. Francis was neither highborn nor lowborn but was part of the growing middle class of merchants, bankers, and artisans—the Minors. Francis did not have the fortune of inheriting a coat of arms; he would have to earn it by fighting and proving his valor on the battlefield.

This was Francis' second experience in battle. During the civil war in the spring of 1198, some four years earlier, the Minors took up arms against the Majors and destroyed the Rocca fortress in a civil war. The castle towering above Assisi represented the old medieval feudal way of life from which the nobility ruled over its citizens.[3]

---

2 Nothing is known about how Francis' father started his business. Whether the grandfather was a poor peasant is speculative; it is a theory stemming from one of the early sources that says that after his conversion, Francis renounced Pietro for Bernardone; i.e., he renounced the wealth of his father to embrace the poverty of his grandfather.

3 The impressive medieval castle, Rocca Maggiore, dominates the Assisi panorama from its steep hilltop position on Mount Subasio. From the Rocca are some breathtaking views of the city and surrounding landscape. It is a reminder of the city's feudal past, as it once stood guard over the city and territory. Its foundations go back at least to ancient Roman times, while in the early Middle Ages (the late ninth century era of the Franks) it served as a stronghold of local barons. After being razed in 1198 by the Minors, the fort passed back and forth between Guelph and Ghibelline factions. It was rebuilt in 1363 by Cardinal Albornoz, and again in 1538 when Assisi was incorporated into the Papal States. Assisi remained under

Armed with swords, pitchforks, and lances, the Minors charged up the mountain toward the castle. Once they arrived, they celebrated to discover the castle already empty. The Count of Assisi, Conrad of Urslingen, had already abandoned the castle. Conrad had served Henry VI, the German emperor, who suddenly died. Now Conrad was quietly en route to Germany, leaving Assisi's Majors to fend for themselves.

Previously, no one would have dared to lift a finger against the fortress, for that would have incurred the wrath of the powerful emperor. But now Henry VI was dead and his heir—a small child—possessed the title of emperor. The Minors took advantage of the untimely death of the emperor and they attacked.

The Minors wasted no time in razing the Rocca of Assisi—the fortress that represented to them centuries of tyrannical feudal rule, keeping them down and out of the power base. They hated the Rocca fortress passionately, as oppressive taxes had been levied against them there and statutes had been drafted granting special privileges to the Majors. The Minors also destroyed the Majors' other fortresses and castles, while most of the Majors fled to nearby Perugia.[4] They then used the stones to reinforce the city walls around Assisi for protection against reprisals from either the Majors or the Perugians.

The Minors promptly declared Assisi an independent commune—a republic free of any feudal domination.

---

the Papal States until 1860 when Italy reunified and Umbria was annexed into the modern Italian Republic. Today the castle is a museum.

4 Perugia is located about twelve miles northwest of Assisi. Today it is one of two principal cities in Umbria.

Commune was the name taken after them, the commoners. They moved the center of government from the Rocca
down to the square near the marketplace in the center
of town where the common people lived.[5] Some Majors
stayed and switched allegiance to the Minors in recognition
of the new government.

One thing was clear: the Rocca—the symbol of feudal-
ism in Assisi—was over. And now the Minors were ruling
Assisi. Yet that did not put an end to the conflict between the
Minors and Majors; it merely exacerbated the animosity.

Unfortunately, war, violence, and cruelty were all too
common in Italy at that time. It went back many centuries.
As the Roman Empire declined in the third and fourth centuries, the spoils of Italy attracted numerous invaders from
beyond the mountains and sea. Assisi was invaded first
by the Byzantines, then the Goths under Totila, then the
Lombards, then the Franks, and finally the Germans.

In order to defend against attacks, the ruling lords organized by surrounding themselves with local nobility and
knights who swore allegiance to fight and protect them,

---

5 Located in the heart of Assisi, the Palazzo del Commune (city hall palace) dates from 1337 and is still in use today as the city hall of Assisi. The
city hall square is known as the Piazza del Commune. The square dates back
to ancient Roman times when it served as a forum and a place of worship, as
the first-century Roman Temple of Minerva once dominated the square. In
medieval times, it was the social, cultural, political, and commercial center
of Assisi. Today it remains largely as it was during the Middle Ages. Next
to it is the Palazzo del Capitano del Popolo (palace of the people's captain), where the chief military commanders of the city resided. The ancient
Foro Romano (Roman forum) is underneath the pavement of the square and
can be visited as a museum; it maintains many ancient and well-preserved
Roman inscriptions, epigraphs, sarcophaguses, and columns.

thereby maintaining peace and order. In return, the noblemen were granted privileges in the form of titles, birthrights, and land possessions. The nobility, in turn, protected
the commoners, allowing them farming rights on their land
from which they could keep some of the produce to live on.
The land, when agreeable, provided for everyone's
needs and was the source of security. As a result, wealth
was concentrated mostly in land. During the feudal era,
wealth and privileges were limited to the few aristocratic
noble landowners, and virtually everyone else was reduced
to a subservient social status. Yet now things had changed
in central Italy and a middle class had developed. Land was
no longer the only source of wealth—money was.

Before the civil war, Francis' father constantly ranted
and raved against the Majors.[6] While Francis was a boy,
he was used to hearing his father moan about them and tell
the story about how they rose to power.

"Those good-for-nothings never did a thing to earn their
money," Pietro often grumbled. "They inherited everything
they owned, which was mostly land. *Boni Homines* they're
called; what a joke! There's not a good man among them!

"Most of their ancestors came down to Italy centuries
ago from the north and with the sword stole our ancestors' land and enslaved us under feudalism. Now they strut
around behind their fancy shields and coats-of-arms, protected by emperors, popes, and other feudal lords. Not one
of them knows a thing about hard work and truly earning
money.

---

6 Pietro is described by the sources in such unpleasant terms as, "hard-
headed, enraged, angry, wrathful, and avaricious."

"Once the barbarian invasions ended two hundred years ago, we were able finally to rebuild the old Roman roads. Then we moved around to buy and sell our merchandise. Yet they make us merchants pay oppressive road tolls as we travel.

"That is how we earned our money. Through our new wealth, we merchants—together with bankers, traders, and artisans—took power away from the land and challenged the Majors. The new economy is now no longer based on land but concentrated in cash and the marketplace.

"Our money was the end of their tyrannical feudalism! One day, the Majors will come to a nasty end! We will tear down their feudal castles and build new communes— independent city-republics governed by us, the people!"

Pietro and his sons were only too eager to participate in the rebellion and watch as most of the nobles were exiled to Perugia.[7] It had been a great day for the Bernardone family and the other Minors of Assisi.

Perhaps Pietro hated the Perugians even more. In that era, people were fiercely loyal to their city. "They are a race of savage warmongers," his father often said. "The Perugians descend from the Etruscans, who taught the Romans a thing or two about war. We Umbrians are peace-loving people. Even though they say the Etruscans were civilized, Umbrians have always been much more cultured."

For a few years after the Assisians had declared independence, there were conflicts with the Perugians over land

---

7 We do not have any historical evidence that Francis participated in this attack, although his family certainly stood to gain much from the demise of the Majors. Many scholars believe Francis did participate in it.

boundaries. Pietro continued: "Those Perugians are the most avaricious race. Do you know how many tolls I have to pay to travel along their roads?

"They are always stealing our best land. I myself have lost some property to them—on our side of the Tiber River no less! Now they are allied with the traitorous Majors."

Pietro was thrilled, then, that his firstborn son was about to fight in a battle that would finally take care of both the Majors and the Perugians.

Francis was not personally very interested in land—or even money. He wanted to be a knight more than anything. He grew up listening to minstrels who meandered through the towns singing *chansons* of damsels who threw roses at audacious lovers.

He never tired of hearing of the deeds of great knights such as Galahad, Arthur, Lancelot, and Tristan. The tales of the knights fired his imagination and filled him with enthusiasm. He dreamed of becoming a hero like them.

Francis was inspired by the ideals of chivalry—of armored knights on horseback, swords and shields, castles and damsels, tournaments, hunts, heraldry, and banners. Knights went out fighting for honor, mercy, courtesy, courage, and justice. Yet they returned to their castles where they enjoyed gala dinners served by a multitude of servants. They enjoyed heaping portions of meats and game with sauces and spices on golden platters and fine wines in diamond-encrusted goblets. There was always banter and bellowing laughter.

Their mottos were the protection of the weakest, *amour*, gallantry toward women, and service to God. Francis would one day enjoy hunting boar and deer in dense forests, he would joust and win tournaments, and he would enjoy dances and music and poetry. This is what he was fighting for.

Francis was not fit to be a merchant, as he quietly believed there was plenty of money and land to go around. His ways had infuriated his father, but Pietro loved his son very much and was always generous with him. Yet he worried that he did not take his life and future seriously.

It had been difficult for Pietro to accept that his firstborn son, to whom his inheritance should rightfully pass, was not fit to be a merchant. But now Pietro was hopeful since Francis had found his calling as a knight. Pietro knew that his son would become great and make him proud yet. And now that day had finally arrived. Assisi would fight Perugia, and Francis would be knighted.

Young Francis was neither a hulking man nor a fierce-looking warrior. His stature was medium to short, and he was of slight build.[8] He had superior skills on a horse and was good with a sword.

But the battle against Perugia did not worry Francis; he believed that the battle was mainly a show of force. Assisi had to mount an impressive campaign to demonstrate its power to the Perugians and the Majors. As part of the cavalry, Francis and the knights would remain safe in the rear, waiting for a break in the line among the Perugian infantry. Then they would charge and attack.

---

8 Thomas of Celano described Francis' appearance: "He was of medium height, closer to short. . . . His neck was slender, his shoulders straight, his arms were short . . . he had thin legs, small feet." Celano, "The Life of Saint Francis," in *Francis of Assisi: Early Documents*, ed. and trans. Regis J. Armstrong, vol. 1, *The Saint* (Hyde Park, NY: New City Press, 1999), chap. 29, 83.

Covered in full armor on his powerful war-horse, Francis felt strong and invincible, and he knew it would be difficult to be severely injured—or worse. As long as the enemy remained in front of him and the Assisian line did not break, he would be fine. There was even a strong probability that Perugia would not even resist, and there would not even be a battle. It could be merely a siege war, where they pounded the walls until Perugia finally surrendered. Either way, Francis was well trained and ready to use his sword.

The Assisians had been preparing for this moment for a long time. The blacksmiths had worked long hours pounding out the armor. The tailors and dyers had sown uniforms. The woodworkers and smiths prepared weapons.

Young men came to fight from the nearby towns and cities of Nocera, Bevagna, Spello, and Rosciano. They, too, had been wronged by Perugia and wanted revenge. Knights came from even farther away. Cavaliers and merchants came from Umbrian cities of Fossato, Nocera, Gubbio, and Fabriano—other cities in perpetual disputes with Perugia over castles and borders.

Francis' father spared no expense in the armor for his son. With the help of a squire, Francis vested in his sleek new steel armor. He mounted an expensive destrier warhorse, which was also armored.

The cathedral bells rang, signaling the call to arms. Seeing the pride in his father's eyes, Francis saluted his parents as he left the family stable and rode to upper Assisi where the army was gathering. Leading the procession-like parade were the trumpeters and drummers followed by townsmen carrying the flag-standards of their respective Assisi quarters: San Rufino, Santa Maria Maggiore, Santa Maria del Sopramuro, Murorotto, Colle, Prato, and San Lorenzo.

They were followed by the guilds: the merchants, shoemakers, butchers, and tax collectors. Then came the infantrymen—the foot soldiers, pike men, spearmen, and archers—all bellowing out Assisian hymns and fight songs. Last of all, slowly and heavily, came the carriage pulled by white oxen draped with the caparison in Assisi's colors of red and blue.

Inside the carriage were the relics of St. Rufino, Assisi's patron saint. San Rufino would protect Assisi and her soldiers. Francis rode with the *Compagnia dei Cavalieri* (the Company of Knights) and vexillifer flag-bearers who closed in the rear.

The army passed through the center of town to the sound of blaring trumpets. Francis and the knights had their metal visors raised. The crowds cheered, and young girls waved kerchiefs at the handsome knights.

Young unmarried women—accompanied by chaperones— offered the young Francis white scarfs, signaling that they were available for marriage. Francis smiled and sensed a deep camaraderie with the knights as if he were already one of them. He felt proud, exhilarated, and powerful.

The army exited through the Porta Antica gate, receiving blessings from the monks of the Benedictine monastery of San Pietro as they passed by. They marched down the road by the *Collis Infernus* (the "Hill of Hell") where criminals were executed and where the same Francis would be buried just twenty-five years later underneath an ornate basilica. The army then marched down toward the plain.

They crossed the bridge near San Vittorino and marched along the Campiglione road that paralleled the Tescio River. As they marched past the Benedictine nuns hidden in their cloister at the monastery of San Paolo, Francis felt their prayers for Assisi's victory, which all believed imminent. They crossed the Chiascio River near Bastia and the road soon merged with the old Via Antica.

At that point, they were in contested territory. The soldiers' mood now changed from jubilant enthusiasm to caution and vigilance. The fight songs died out and they became quiet.

They soon approached the Tiber River from the small village of Collestrada, known for the leper hospital on the hill. Now they were just a few miles from the Perugian city walls.[9] Once they crossed the river at Ponte San Giovanni (St. John's Bridge), they would be fully in Perugian territory.

When about half the army had crossed the bridge, Francis heard shouting and clamoring behind him. With his bulky headgear and clanging armor, it was difficult to discern what was happening. He was about to turn his horse around and look when he heard someone yell, "Ambush!"

Francis then saw Perugian soldiers swarming out of the dense forest on both sides of the road. They had been betrayed! He unsheathed his sword.

---

9 Collestrada and Ponte San Giovanni are in close proximity to one another and lie halfway between Assisi and Perugia. "The Legend of the Three Companions," in *Francis of Assisi: Early Documents*, ed. and trans. Regis J. Armstrong, vol. 2, *The Founder* (Hyde Park, NY: New City Press, 2000), chap. 1, is the only early source to mention this battle, but does not name the location. Historians have ascertained that it took place in this area. Today Collestrada is known for its large shopping mall.

The Assisian army was scattered in all directions in complete disarray. The battle raged across the hill and the forest. It extended up to the Collestrada castle and even spilled into the lepers' hospital.

Francis' first biographer, Thomas of Celano, would later say that it was a bloodbath beyond every measure. Other chroniclers spoke of a long battle, severe slaughter, rivers flowing with blood, separated body parts. In the end, the Assisians were soundly defeated. When word of the massacre reached Assisi, the streets were loud with wailing as its citizens wept for their husbands, cousins, sons, brothers, and fathers.

Some survivors were bound and taken away to Perugia. Francis was one of them. As he looked around at the dead and wounded who lay disfigured in the fields, his desire to become a knight died as well. He would not become great after all.

Francis would spend a full year in the dungeon in Perugia. There he witnessed the utter brutality that human beings were capable of inflicting on one another. Francis was spared the most savage tortures because he was well armored and was riding with the knights; the Perugians mistakenly believed he was part of the nobility. They used him and the other noblemen as leverage in negotiations and for ransom.

The others were not so fortunate. Under the Perugian banner of the griffin—a mythical creature with the body of a lion and the head and wings of an eagle—Francis watched helplessly as his fellow combatants were tortured inhumanely. As a show of victory, Perugia's citizens looked on in delight to see their hated enemies paraded through the city of Perugia. They were publically hung in gibbet hanging cages, whipped, branded, and dragged through the streets while tied to horses.

Then they were thrown in an underground prison where the tortures only increased. Sadistic guards hoisted up their prisoners onto the rack by their hands and feet and pulled out their teeth, they stuffed toads in their mouths, they interred prisoners alive, they cut off their noses and other extremities.

It was heartless and merciless. Francis had never experienced anything as cruel and savage as what he experienced in Perugia.[10] One year later, Francis' father paid the ransom, and Francis was free to come home.

---

10 Nothing is known historically about how the Assisian prisoners of war were treated in Perugia. The tortures I have listed were commonly used on prisoners of battle in Italy at that time.

3

FROM WAR TO
OBEDIENCE IN SPOLETO

My son, if you receive my words and treasure my commands, Turning your ear to wisdom, inclining your heart to understanding . . . then will you understand the fear of the Lord; the knowledge of God you will find.

Proverbs 2:1–2, 5 NABRE

A tattered, emaciated, and broken man returned to Assisi. Francis had picked up an illness in the squalid Perugian prison and was often tired. Normally, Francis was cheerful and vivacious. But not anymore.

Instead, he was sullen and stayed home most of the time. He slept often, though no amount of rest was able to relieve his inner fatigue. He even stayed away from the sumptuous feasts with his old companions.

The battle of Collestrada and a year in prison had changed something deep within Francis. His experience of the horrors of war, human butchery, and time spent in that dank, subterranean, gloomy dungeon had crushed his normally jovial disposition and bright personality. His parents worried about him, especially his mother, Pica. His father just wanted to see him regain motivation and do something important with his life. Francis, too, wondered deep down

if he really had been called to be great or if the prophecy
had been wishful youthful fantasy.

One morning, a companion poked his head in his father's
shop where Francis was seated at a desk going through
some ledgers. He was once again working for Pietro. "Hey,
Francesco, did you hear the news from the town crier this
morning?" he asked.

Francis had not. He remained quietly seated at his desk
with his head buried in his work. His buddy filled him in:
"Men from all over Europe are going south to Apulia to
join Sir Walter of Brienne to fight for the pope for control of southern Italy against the excommunicated German
emperor, Otto, and his troops. Could be your chance for
redemption, eh?"

With a smirk on his face, his cohort left. Francis sat up
and reflected for a moment. Go to war again? To fight for
Sir Walter on behalf of Pope Innocent III would surely be
a noble cause.

But he still lacked strength and was not well. His desire
for knighthood had been quashed. No . . . no way, not
again, not now. He turned his attention back to his work
and quickly forgot the conversation.

That evening, Francis went to sleep and recalled what
his friend said. As he fell asleep, he heard a strange voice—
one he had never heard before. The voice said that he
would marry a most beautiful bride and become the lord of
a magnificent palace filled with knightly arms and glitter-
ing shields, and many knights would follow him.[1]

---

1 See Bonaventure of Bagnoregio, "The Major Legend of Saint Francis,"
in *Francis of Assisi: Early Documents*, ed. and trans. Regis J. Armstrong,

Francis sat up in bed, startled and fully awake. What did the voice mean? What kind of dream was it? Was it a sign that he was destined to fight and lead others in battle? Would he become a wealthy knight after all? Would he become great?

Francis did not fall back asleep as he reflected on these things for the rest of the night. He thought of fighting for a lord and of the formula of knightly consecration: "In the name of God, of St. George, and of St. Michael, I make you a knight. Be proud, courageous, faithful."

His desire for knighthood began to come back—just a little. Even though he did not feel totally convinced in his heart, he concluded that the dream was a sign that he was to return to the battlefield and become a knight after all. Yes, he would fight once again, he thought.

"I know that I am going to be a great prince," he said to himself.[2] "I will do great things yet. The prophecy will still be fulfilled."

After Francis announced his intentions to his family, his father was hopeful but cautious. Yet he once again commissioned the construction of fine armor and purchased the best war-horse for his son. Francis' mother, Pica, however, was gravely worried and was not supportive. But Pietro did not want to hear her, and he blasted her.

---

vol. 2, *The Founder* (Hyde Park, NY: New City Press, 2000), chap. 1, 3; and Thomas of Celano, "The Remembrance of the Desire of a Soul," in *Francis of Assisi: Early Documents*, vol. 2, *The Founder*, chap. 2, 6.

2 See St. Francis, "The Beginning or the Founding of the Order and the Deeds of Those Lesser Brothers Who Were the First Companions of the Blessed Francis in Religion," in *Francis of Assisi: Early Documents*, vol. 2, *The Founder*, chap. 1, 5.

The morning Francis prepared to depart, his father looked sternly into his eyes. There were no sentimental words, just a command—almost a threat: "Do not disappoint me, son. You are a son of the Bernardone family, and I still believe that you will bring honor to this family! Our family is strong! Never forget that!"

As Francis prepared to depart, there were no ceremonies, no festivities, no parades—just Francis and a few older knights setting out quietly through the San Rufino gate. Francis knew their stories as soon as he saw them. They were mercenaries and were in it for the money.

He had fought with mercenaries with the Assisian army in the battle against Perugia. These old knights had the same worn faces and rough, leathery skin, telling of years of riotous living. Their eyes had that stony gaze and icy stare, revealing a hardened and empty soul.

They had once believed in and fought for great ideals, but now they were embittered and apathetic. It made no difference to them if they were fighting for the pope or the emperor, for one city or the other. They had been in battles and had killed and maimed many people, probably even off the battlefield. Francis felt uneasy.

It would be a long journey south to Apulia, in excess of two weeks. They would take the road through St. Sabinus to Foligno, then the Via Flaminia to Rome, and finally the ancient Roman Via Appia—the queen of the roads—down to Apulia. The sound of the horses' clip-clop on the road reminded Francis of the days he spent caravanning with his father up to France to purchase merchandise.

He thought of all the delights he had seen at the fairs in the city of Champagne: gold, silver, ivory, fine pearls, tapestries, rugs and furs, warehouses and counters full of silk and velvet, oriental spices and perfumes. The bellowing laughter and boisterous stories told by his father and the other gregarious merchants made the long, arduous trips pleasurable. They were accompanied by well-trained guards and Francis had always felt safe.

Now, however, it was quiet and no one said much. And even though he was traveling with knights who were much more dangerous than his father's guards, Francis felt much more vulnerable and insecure.

"Where am I? Where am I going? What am I doing here?" Francis kept asking himself over and over as they traveled farther and farther away from his home in Assisi. The deep loneliness within him grew and grew. He felt terrible. "Where is my greatness now?" he asked himself.

It was nighttime when they arrived in Spoleto, where they prepared to overnight.[3] This was the capital city of the dukedom that had controlled Assisi just a few years earlier, but it was now subject to the Papal States of Pope Innocent III. Francis' thoughts were firing too rapidly for him to sleep, and he just lay there staring at the stars in the sky.

Just as there was so much conflict and upheaval in society, so was there a lack of peace in his heart. He felt the anxiety in his stomach grow, and he feared another sleepless night. He would need strength for the journey and battles ahead.

Francis was convinced that what he was doing was right. It was confirmed in the dream. He was going to Apulia to

---

3 Spoleto is located about forty-five miles south of Assisi. Today it is an important Umbrian city known for an international arts festival. It is known for its well-preserved medieval and ancient historic center, including an aqueduct and bridge with Roman origins.

fight and become a knight. But why fight again? For glory? For greatness?

Before the battle against Perugia, he had wanted to become a knight more than anything. But now he was not so sure. He had previously romanticized war, but the only battle in which he had actually fought showed him its gruesome reality. He saw people do horrible things to one another on the field, after the battle, and in the prison. War no longer seemed glorious or noble to him.

Was he supposed to kill? Was it just? Yes, he would be fighting on behalf of the pope against the excommunicated German emperor. But was he actually supposed to raise the sword? Was there another way?

He began to wonder if he had ever experienced true peace or joy. For most of his life, he had known the thrill of excitement, pleasure, and exhilaration. Did those things bring him peace? His former ways filled his heart—or at least he thought they did. Francis used to think of himself as a peaceful person, but now he had anguish in his heart. Maybe he had never been peaceful.

What was peace? Would he ever have it in his heart? Would he ever be serene? Would he ever be joyful? He started to believe that he was making a huge mistake. His conscience was not right.

His thoughts intuitively turned to God. Francis was Catholic, and he had been baptized and raised in a Catholic home. Catholicism was deeply intertwined with his society and culture.

Francis had been educated at the parish school of San Giorgio, where the priests catechized him in the faith in addition to teaching him arithmetic and basic Latin.

As a young man, he had never rejected God . . . but true religion had never been important to him on a personal level.

He thought of the priests at his school. They always said that Jesus was the true Lord and that Christians should serve him and him alone. While some of his teachers were severe, others exuded a truly peaceful presence from within. Why were they peaceful? What was different about them? Francis was ruminating on all these things as he drifted off to sleep.

As he lay there half asleep, he heard the voice again. It was the same voice that had recently spoken to him, telling him that he would marry a beautiful bride and become lord of a great palace. This time, however, it said, "Francis, who can do more for you, the lord or his servant, a rich man or a beggar?"

Francis had heard numerous voices that competed for his attention his entire life, but this time he knew it was the voice of God. This time, for the first time in his life, Francis listened to the voice of God.

The answer to the question was easy in the still largely feudalistic society in which he had grown up. People were ranked according to class or profession— one was either noble or a commoner; one always served someone higher and was served, in turn, by someone lower. Peasants served landlords who served knights who served counts who served dukes who served popes or emperors.

Francis responded to the voice that a lord or a rich man could do more. Then the voice asked another question: "Then why are you serving the servant?"

Francis sat up, wide awake. Whom had he been serving? He pondered that question. It confused him. Had he not been serving God?

Francis never thought he had ever actually rejected God. In fact, he believed that he had been serving God, for a knight's motto was "My soul to God, my life to the king, my heart to my lady, honor to me." If he was not actually serving God, then whom was he serving?

Francis began to consider that perhaps he had not been serving the true Lord. Maybe he had been serving someone or something else. Francis then asked the voice, "Lord, what do you want me to do?" The voice responded, "Go back to your home and you will be shown what to do."[4]

Should he actually turn back to Assisi? What about the other dream when he was told he would become a great knight and military commander? What about his childhood prophecy?

How would he become a great prince now? Had he misinterpreted the first dream? Was the Devil playing tricks on him?

There would be huge consequences to pay if he turned back to Assisi. Everyone would judge him as a coward. This would bring tremendous shame to his family, especially his father.

It was one thing to lose on the battlefield and be imprisoned with everyone else—but to just turn back and quit?

---

4 See Bonaventure, "Major Legend," chap. 1, 3. Bonaventure presents the second vision/dream as a turning point for Francis in which he becomes obedient to the will of God: "When morning came, then, he returned in haste to Assisi, free of care and filled with joy, and, already made an exemplar of obedience, he awaited the Lord's will."

What would his father do to him? Would he disinherit him?

It was a long night as Francis tried to sort out all these things in his mind. He meditated deeply and reflected on stories of Jesus.

Suddenly Francis remembered a Gospel story. He recalled Jesus with his disciples in Gethsemane. As the soldiers came to arrest Jesus, Peter drew his sword. He was acting naturally as a knight in service and defense of his Lord, the holy innocent One. But Jesus rebuked Peter, saying, "Put your sword back into its place; for all who take the sword will perish by the sword" (Mt 26:52).

Why would Jesus choose to be defenseless and vulnerable in front of his aggressors? Why would he command Peter *not* to protect him? Jesus knew they were going to arrest, torture, and crucify him.

This was one of those stories about Jesus that had always seemed contradictory and counterintuitive to Francis, to the point of seeming unbelievable. It was similar to other Gospel passages, such as when Jesus said, "Love your enemies, do good to those who hate you, bless those who curse you, pray for those who abuse you. To him who strikes you on the cheek, offer the other also" (Lk 6:27–29).

What was it about Jesus? What did he understand that practically no one else did? What did he mean during his interrogation with Pontius Pilate before his execution when he said, "My kingdom does not belong to this world. If my kingdom did belong to this world, my attendants [would] be fighting to keep me from being handed over to the Jews. But as it is, my kingdom is not here" (Jn 18:36 NABRE)?

What was the kingdom of God? What was the glory of God? Why did Jesus say, "The last will be first, and the first last" (Mt 20:16)?

Francis soon began to consider that Jesus' ways were very different from the ways of the world. For the first time in his life, Francis began to have an inkling of who the true Lord really was and what it meant to be a true Christian. He then understood that he had been living his life in search of earthly rewards with no understanding of heavenly glory.

At that moment, Francis became dramatically aware of his pride and sinfulness. It became clear to him that he had been separated from God up to that point in his life through his disobedience. Francis had not understood that the Lord was jealous and demanded to be worshipped and served alone: "Hear, O Israel: The LORD our God is one LORD; and you shall love the LORD your God with all your heart, and with all your soul, and with all your might" (Dt 6:4–5).

It was clear to Francis that he was to obey God before all else. God was to be Francis' only Lord, and he was to have no other gods. Although he knew of the commandments, Francis now recognized in the First Commandment that God was the source of all love and life.

At that moment in Spoleto, God was calling Francis to obedience. He was to accept him and worship him alone: "This is why you must now acknowledge, and fix in your heart, that the LORD is God in the heavens above and on earth below, and that there is no other" (Dt 4:39 NABRE).

Francis then made a decision to give his entire life and will to God in an act of obedience. He did not care if he would become a great prince or not. He made a decision to place his faith and trust in God, even if at that point Francis did not yet know God well.

For Francis, this was the beginning of wisdom, his fear of the Lord (cf. Prv 9:10; Ps 111:10). Yet this was also the beginning of his freedom. Francis' obedience would eventually restore him to the kingdom of heaven, and the chasm that existed between God and him would soon be reconciled through Christ. In obedience to God, Francis' life would become properly and correctly ordered.

The question posed to Francis by God there in Spoleto, "Whom are you serving?," was essentially the same one God had asked someone else once before when he queried the first man, Adam, "Where are you?" (cf. Gn 3:9). It is the same question that God poses to all people whenever they are lost and are not seeking to conform their will to his will.

Geographically, Francis was in Spoleto on the way to fight in a crusade. Yet spiritually, Francis was far from God and was not serving him. With proper introspection and discernment, God was giving Francis another chance; he had the choice to change direction, learn how to serve him, and become obedient.

From Spoleto on, Francis would seek to know and love God. He would seek to break the bond of disobedience he had inherited from Adam. And he would submit himself in obedience to God as reconciled through Christ.

He would strive to listen to and discern the voice of God for the rest of his life, asking God what he wanted him to do, and he would seek to love the Lord with all his heart, with all his soul, and with all his mind (cf. Mt 22:37).

Francis was finished eating the rotten fruit of the tree of disobedience and self-will. Instead, he would now eat from the banquet of the eternal tree of obedience and God's will.

Francis would choose Jesus' way—the way of the Gospels. He would put down the sword forever and return to Assisi regardless of the consequences. The decision to follow the Lord back to Assisi put his conscience at rest and greatly eased the anxiety he felt inside.

Francis felt confident that he was moving in the right direction. This was the first time in his life that Francis listened to the voice of God and discerned God's will correctly. He would spend the rest of his life seeking to respond correctly to the question "Whom are you serving?"

The next morning, Francis announced to the knights that he was turning back. None seemed surprised. Francis offered his mantle, armor, and horse to the poorest knight.

He was like another St. Martin of Tours, who some eight centuries earlier had cut his military mantle in two with his sword, giving half to a beggar. Or perhaps he was like Saul on the road to Damascus (see Acts 9:3–9). Either way, he turned around and went back to Assisi. The knights left without saying a word to him and continued their drive toward war.

4

HUMILITY AND
SAN DAMIANO

Whoever exalts himself will be humbled, and whoever humbles himself will be exalted.

MATTHEW 23:12

ONCE back in Assisi, Francis wanted to be alone. He was tired of making excuses and avoiding people. He wanted to get away from all the gossip and whispering about him.

His father was exasperated and did not know what to do. Francis was not sure if he would ever be able to mend that relationship, as he had caused Pietro so much shame and disgrace. He knew with his whole heart that he was supposed to be back in Assisi—that is what the voice told him to do—but he still did not understand why.

Francis was feeling sadness again. Not even the beautiful landscape of the Spoleto valley, the beauty of the fields, or the pleasant vineyards—all of which he usually took great delight in—could lift his spirits.[1] Francis was

---

1 Cf. Thomas of Celano, "The Life of Saint Francis," in *Francis of Assisi: Early Documents*, ed. and trans. Regis J. Armstrong, vol. 1, *The Saint* (Hyde Park, NY: New City Press, 1999), chap. 2, 3. However, Thomas

now feeling strongly tempted again to believe that he was a failure, that his life was a waste, that he was worth nothing. He thought of the prophecy once again that he would be a great prince. "What kind of prince will I become now?" he wondered to himself.

Now he just wanted to be quiet and stay by himself. Francis had a companion who accompanied him to the caves and ruined sanctuaries in the hills and valley around Assisi.[2] There Francis prayed in solace and felt free to be himself—whoever or whatever that was.

He was particularly fond of a little church dedicated to the two physician brothers—Sts. Damian and Cosmas. The church, known locally simply as San Damiano, had originally been built over an old pagan shrine.[3] More recently, it

places Francis' sullenness before he has the dream to go to Apulia, while I place it after he returns from Spoleto to Assisi.

2 Thomas of Celano says, "Now there was in the city of Assisi a man he loved more than all the rest. They were of the same age and the constant intimacy of their mutual love made him bold to share his secrets with him. He often brought him to remote places suitable for talking, asserting that he had found a great and valuable treasure. This man was overjoyed, and since he was so excited about what he heard, he gladly went with him whenever he was summoned." Celano, "Life of Saint Francis," chap. 3, 6. The man is never named; some biographers (e.g., Sabatier and Jorgensen) believe the companion to be Brother Elias. Also, the place of introspection is not known. Thomas of Celano in the above reference says it was in a "cave near the city." Therefore, Fortini believes this place of introspection and conversion happened in the Carceri caves, while I place it in San Damiano.

3 San Damiano is a lovely sanctuary about one mile from the city walls. It stands on the hillside where St. Felicianus (the patron saint of nearby Foligno) was, according to tradition, exiled from Assisi in the third century after preaching. Located among the groves of olive trees, San Damiano preserves some of the most important memories of the Franciscan story. When Francis arrived, it was just a small country church with a building behind

had served as a hospital for pilgrims and crusaders passing through the area on their way south to Rome and beyond.

Now, however, it was neglected and in disrepair. An old priest named Father Peter resided there who was about as tattered as the church.[4] He did his best to keep the place up; however, he was no longer young and strong. Just the same, he still celebrated for the handful of local peasants who came to Mass on Sundays and Holy Days.

Just a few years earlier, Francis never would have entered a church like this, even if it had been in good condition. Those old, squatty churches, dimly illuminated by oil lamps with low ceilings, broad rounded arches, and thick walls, seemed too dreary and reminded him of burial tombs. Back then, he admired the sleek new cathedrals going up in the cities in France.

While traveling with his father, he was mesmerized by architects' ability to engineer the high ceilings with the tall, thin walls supported by flying buttresses. Those churches were fresh and innovative: the colored, stained-glass windows rendered the naves bright and vibrant. The soaring spires, pointed arches, high walls, steep roofs, and incense all went up, which was the direction he was going in his life.

---

it. St. Clare later lived there for over forty years with her sisters. Today San Damiano is a sanctuary designated exclusively as a place of prayer.

4 *Anonymous of Perugia* is the only early source to name the priest. See St. Francis, "The Beginning or the Founding of the Order and the Deeds of Those Lesser Brothers Who Were the First Companions of the Blessed Francis in Religion," in *Francis of Assisi: Early Documents*, ed. and trans. Regis J. Armstrong, vol. 2, *The Founder* (Hyde Park, NY: New City Press, 2000), chap. 1, 7.

Now, ironically, Francis felt some peace in this broken-down Church of San Damiano. The collapsing church was just like his life. Its bricks had crumbled just as had his dream of becoming a knight.

Francis' values, hopes, and aspirations for his life were all gone now. His inner spirit felt as musty and dank as the interior of the church. The old paintings and frescoes were like his hope for the future—faded and gray. The droppings on the floor from the birds nesting in the beams represented what he thought of himself.

What did God really want? he asked himself. Why did God tell him to go back to Assisi? What was God's will? Would he ever be a prince? Francis felt the anguish and torment begin to return inside.

One thing in particular captivated his attention inside the church: the crucifix.[5] He was drawn to stare up at that large, wooden, Byzantine cross that filled the small nave. Francis once again drew on his religion.

Francis knew a little about God, but he had not yet experienced a personal encounter with God. Francis had no significant relationship with him at that point. Effectively,

---

5 Icons have been used as objects of religious devotion since at least the second century. In an era of illiteracy, icons, pictures, and statues told stories, much as we read books today. Medieval people would "read" paintings, which were filled with symbolism, figures, allegory, and signs that they would have understood. Color, position of objects, animals, clothing, landscape, proportion, haloes, numbers, and light all had meaning. Icons depicted spiritual, not physical, realities; thus, the images were not intended to be realistic. In the Byzantine period, there was an emphasis on depicting the risen Christ (*Christus Triumphans*). In the later Middle Ages and Renaissance, artists shifted toward realism and Christ was depicted as suffering, limp, or slumping (*Christus Patiens*).

his relationship with Christianity was cultural, and his religious observance took the form of what was expected of him.

Sure, he went to church on Sundays and Holy Days, but his prayers were mostly rote. Religion was about custom, decorum, and decency. He was religious because everyone else was religious; he was Catholic to the same degree that he was Assisian, Umbrian, and Italian. God, for him, was still a vague being somewhere up in heaven far away.

Francis recalled the dream in Spoleto: serving the Lord. Since he had nothing else to turn to, he decided to pray. He gazed up at the crucifix. On that cross, Francis saw a man who had suffered just as he was suffering now.[6] Christ's wounds in his hands, feet, and side were marked very clearly with large black holes, from which blood was flowing. Francis felt as if he, too, were attached to a cross that had bloodied his own hands, feet, and side. He recalled the Cistercian preachers' detailed sermons of Christ's passion and crucifixion as they preached in Assisi on Good Friday some time earlier.[7] At the time, their words were hollow and insignificant to Francis, since he had never really

---

6 The Christ on the San Damiano crucifix is not depicted suffering, *Christus Patiens*; rather, he is resurrected, *Christus Triumphans*. Most depictions of Christ on the crucifix at and before the time of Francis were of him resurrected. In fact, in the thirteenth century and later, the Franciscans and other mendicant orders promoted the image of the suffering Christ as a popular devotion. Here I depicted Francis focusing on Christ's sufferings because I am emphasizing him experiencing that at this time in his life.

7 The Cistercians were a recent offshoot from the Benedictine Order beginning in 1098 when twenty-one monks left their monastery in Burgundy, France. They felt that the Benedictine way of life had abandoned the penance and simplicity of the Rule of St. Benedict. They embraced a simple

experienced suffering. But now, the memories of their sermons struck Francis deeply. Francis realized that up until that point, he had fled the cross, and consequently Jesus, his entire life.

Francis began to feel a connection to the man on the cross. He began to feel that he could approach the cross regardless of what he had done. The cross did not care if he had committed the most wicked, vile, and reprehensible mortal sins or if he was guilty of a mere handful of venial infractions. Christ took all sins onto himself through the cross. It was a gift completely undeserved by Francis. There was absolutely nothing Francis could have done to deserve the gift of Christ's sacrifice for him. It was unconditional and Francis had only to accept it.

Francis soon began to connect with Jesus' suffering. Or perhaps it was *Jesus* connecting with *Francis'* suffering. In any case, Francis began to enter into the mystery of Christ's passion and suffering through his own suffering. He could not understand it; he could only reflect on it and meditate on it. He could only receive and accept the cross; it was not his to conquer. Despite the paradox, the cross somehow gave meaning, value, and sense to the pain Francis was experiencing.

Francis started to change. He began to experience the Lord deep within. He soon sensed that God was not angry with him but loved him deeply.

In the cross, Francis found forgiveness, and he soon began to impute all the sins he had ever done onto the cross.

---

life of work in the fields, love, prayer, and self-denial. Some went out and preached Christ's poverty and passion.

In the past, Francis had wondered why or how God could be forgiving, as forgiveness had always seemed to him a sign of weakness or feebleness. But now he came to realize that God forgave through Christ in order to free people for a much greater experience of love.

Because of God's forgiveness of each person, Francis could also learn to forgive others as well as himself. He realized that God was most concerned with showing his great love and mercy. Now Francis understood how God desires mercy and not sacrifice (cf. Mt 9:13; Hos 6:6). And God wanted Francis to imitate that same love.

In his encounter with God through the crucifix, Francis was being transformed. His heart soon came alive with a burning, consuming love. God was moving from a distant place up in heaven somewhere to a loving place deep within Francis' heart. The cross was Francis' initiation into the spiritual life; it was his starting point. Of course, Francis had no idea at that point that the cross would be his ending point, too, as he would receive its imprint on his body shortly before his death in Laverna.

Francis began coming to San Damiano often for prayer before the crucifix. He began to love the cross very much. He would sit quietly before the cross without saying or doing anything. He would leave everything behind—his thoughts, his ideas, even his hopes and expectations for the future.

Francis simply sought to get quiet with God in calmness and stillness with nothing but the cross. And in that intimate time spent with God, God began to speak to him. The sense of separation from God and others began to leave him, and he began to feel a sense of oneness with God, people, and even all creation.

That sense of inner shame and sinfulness that had always had a grip on him at some level also began to leave him. In fact, it became very clear to him that it was the sin at his core that had driven him to do the things he did. He had been seeking to liberate himself, even if unconsciously, from his inner ugliness—his sin.

So great was his awareness of the sin within him that he began to consider himself the greatest of all sinners. Francis did not actually believe that he was the worst sinner in the world; rather, his use of the superlative was his way of expressing just how profound and radical his own sense of sin was. And the awareness of the profundity of his sin caused him to place *all* his faith and reliance upon *God*, no longer on himself. He was now filling and reforming his sinful soul with God's *grace* instead of seeking his own will in an effort to try to wrest some happiness and satisfaction from the world. In seeking his own will, he received shame and confusion, while in seeking God's will, he began to experience grace and peace.

Francis confessed frequently to Peter at San Damiano and received the Eucharist from him. He learned much about religion and spiritual things from him. Francis began reflecting on the Scriptures. He was particularly struck by the Beatitudes, by Jesus' exaltation of humble things. He compared what he was learning about God to his former way of life when he was always trying to improve his lot.

Before, he had always tried to fashion himself in the latest and best clothes; he was always seeking better companions, the most beautiful girl to marry—the higher born the better. He had tried to move up the social ladder by becoming a knight. Always more prestige, more power, greater glory, up, up, up. Such ideals seemed very different from the Christ on the cross upon whom Francis was gazing—the God who was going down, down, down.

Religion was now making sense to Francis. He was slowly discovering something new in his life. It was very different from anything he had ever experienced. This was the true Jesus of the Gospels. Ultimately, it had taken deep suffering in order for Francis to truly connect with Jesus and become genuinely religious.

One day, while he was gazing at the crucifix, something caught Francis' attention. It began to rain, and he noticed water enter the church through the broken roof. He watched the water as it dripped down and splashed on the pavement.

As it pooled up, the water spread out and seeped into the cracks in the floor. The water began running down the uneven floor to the lowest part. It flowed outside the church and seeped down into the ground.

The nature of water, Francis noticed, is to go down. He looked at Jesus on the crucifix—his blood was dripping down, going lower. . . . Suddenly Francis had an inspiration: God is like water! God goes down! To the lowest part!

A Scripture passage raced through Francis' mind: "Qui, cum in forma Dei esset, non rapinam arbitratus est esse se aequalem Deo, sed semetipsum exinanivit formam servi accipiens, in similtudinem hominum factus" (Phil 2:6–7; Who, though he was in the form of God, did not count equality with God a thing to be grasped, but emptied himself, taking the form of a servant, being born in the likeness of men).[8] At that moment, Francis fully understood the meaning of that text.

For Jesus, it would have been "robbery" to keep to himself what was his—that is, his divinity and his highest position in heaven. It was against the nature of the Word to grasp jealously or cling to his royal position in heaven, though that was, indeed, his right. What a mystery that almighty God humbled himself by coming down from heaven's royal throne (cf. Ws 18:15) and taking on human flesh in the womb of a virgin.

Christ chose to relinquish his divine glory and take on a lesser form. He lowered himself, emptied himself, humbled himself, and became incarnate precisely because *he is love*. The nature of divinity, therefore, is to give—indeed, to love.

This was love: to sacrifice, to humble, to give of one's self, to move outwards toward the other. For God, it meant becoming something that was less than himself. It meant Divinity becoming humanity, the Creator becoming the created.

It was an awesome mystery that the incarnation of God did not manifest himself in great glory. For Christ did not appear as an emperor or king, though he was the King of kings! He did not become incarnate as a great lord, though he was the Lord of lords! He did not arrive in clouds of glory; instead, he came as a defenseless child, born in an insignificant place and surrounded by common animals.

He needed to be cared for and protected by his poor mother and adopted father. Joseph, a carpenter, was a

---

8 The Greek and Latin scriptural texts used a word for "robbery" in this passage. The original word gives it stronger meaning.

craftsman whose social position was not among the nobility; he was a commoner, a minor. Even Francis' own social status as a commoner himself—a merchant—was greater than that of the craftsman.

But perhaps more revealing of the nature of God was how Jesus' earthly life ended: "Et habitu inventus ut homo, humiliavit semetipsum factus oboediens usque ad mortem, mortem autem cruces" (Phil 2:8; And being found in human form he humbled himself and became obedient unto death, even death on a cross). Christ humbled himself—going all the way down to the lowest, most humiliating place possible, in excruciating pain—to the cross to take humanity's sins.

Criminals convicted of serious offenses were the lowliest, most despised in Francis' era, and Jesus, the Son of God himself, stooped to their status. Yet the Lord of lords was not content to stop there, and he continued lower still. After his death, he went as far down as possible—into the depths of hell to Sheol, Hades—to free the just who had gone before him. By going all the way down into hell, Christ humbled himself to the lowest place possible.

And yet, the humble things that the Lord had done some twelve centuries before Francis' life were not one-time historical events. Francis thought of the Eucharist: still then, God continued to humble and reveal himself in the little form of bread and wine. Daily he still came in humble form—daily he still came down from the bosom of the Father upon the altar in the hands of the priest. That the Lord of the universe, God and the Son of God, so humbled himself that for Francis' salvation, he hid himself under the little form of bread![9]

---

9 Cf. St. Francis, "A Letter to the Entire Order," in *Francis and Clare: The Complete Works*, trans. Regis J. Armstrong (Mahwah, NJ: Paulist

These ideas fired Francis' imagination. God continually gives of himself, goes down, and makes himself lesser—*minor*! God is *minor*! What a paradox—that the almighty, all-powerful, all-knowing, omnipotent God of the universe humbled and emptied himself of the glories of heaven to become human!

Francis now understood that he had been looking in the wrong direction. He had been looking up his entire life in search of earthly glory when God was looking down in order to show Francis and all of humanity heavenly glory!

While joyfully reflecting on these mysteries, Francis looked outside the little Church of San Damiano and noticed several larks walking around on the ground. The birds were scavenging for food. Then the birds suddenly flew up and away.

They darted back and forth, flying higher and higher. Eventually they became mere brown dots, smaller and smaller in the immensity of the white sky. And then they were gone.

The birds gave Francis great hope. As Francis looked up at the crucifix in the little ruined Church of San Damiano, he no longer saw one who was suffering. Now he saw Jesus standing on the cross in serene majesty and glory. On the cross, Christ—the second Person of the Trinity in the form of a man—was resurrected from his bloody wounds and death. He had overcome his passion and suffering. He was resurrected!

Press, 1982), 26–29; and St. Francis, "The Admonitions," in *Francis and Clare: The Complete Works*, chap. 1, for more on Francis' ideas regarding the Eucharist and humility.

Suffering was not the final condition, the Resurrection was! After water seeped down into the ground, it, too, eventually evaporated and, like the larks, returned back up to the sky. Not only did God go down; he eventually went back up.

In that crucifix, Francis saw that Jesus, who had been rich in heaven, made himself poor among men, who are materially rich but spiritually poor, so that people could inherit the divine riches of the kingdom of heaven.[10] He took on our human poverty to give people divine riches. Francis continued reflecting on Scripture: "Propter quod et Deus illum exaltavit et donavit illi nomen, quod est super omne omen, ut in nomine Iesu omne genu flectatur caelestium et terrestrium et infernorum et omnis lingua confiteatur: 'Dominus Iesus Christus!', in gloriam Dei Patris" (Phil 2:9–11; Therefore God has highly exalted him and bestowed on him the name which is above every name, that at the name of Jesus every knee should bow, in heaven and on earth and under the earth, and every tongue confess that Jesus Christ is Lord, to the glory of God the Father).

Christ humbled himself by becoming like us and taking on great sufferings because of his great love! Francis realized that God would indeed raise people up, but not without going down first. Francis had always sought to be exalted; he had always tried to propel himself up in worldly ways through his own volition, with his own power. Now

---

10 See St. Francis, "The Second Version of the Letter to the Faithful," in *Francis and Clare: The Complete Works*, 4–15, for an expansion on these ideas.

he realized that he did *not* have the power to raise himself up—only God did through the Holy Spirit. Francis would allow God to raise him up in *God's* way, not *Francis'*, for "God opposes the proud, but gives grace to the humble" (1 Pt 5:5).

From then on, Francis would seek to embrace the humble things on earth in order to be raised up and receive spiritual rewards in heaven. He had finally found direction for his life on earth: *down.* He would cease self-seeking through worldly honors.

On the contrary, he would now seek to become minor by imitating Jesus, embracing the cross, and going down. And by doing so, he had faith that, like Jesus, he would be raised up. True to his baptismal name, John, Francis then realized that he was not called to become a prince of this world; rather, he would become a spiritual prince. His motto would become "Humble yourselves therefore under the mighty hand of God, that in due time he may exalt you" (1 Pt 5:6).

Francis looked up at the crucifix again. Though it was the same cross, it seemed a little different. Just for a moment, Francis thought, it seemed that Jesus was smiling.

5

LEPROSY AND MINORITY

When he saw [the lepers] he said to them, "Go and show yourselves to the priests." And as they went they were cleansed.

LUKE 17:14

F RANCIS set out from Assisi on horseback toward his father's property near the country Church of San Pietro della Spina in the valley just past the area of Rivotorto, known as the "crooked stream." His father owned a building there for dying clothes. Francis was once again working for his father, even though they were not getting along. He was often absentminded at work, and his father had become increasingly impatient with him.

The soon-to-be saint left Assisi through the Moiano city gate and traveled down past the monastery of San Masseo to the Via Antiqua—the ancient road connecting Rome with France and northern Europe.[1] From there he would pass by Arce toward Castelnuovo and then take the Via

---

1 The name of this road was recently changed to "Via Francesca" (the French Road) as it was an important road in Francis' era linking Foligno and Perugia and then continuing on toward Siena where it joined the ancient Via Francigena which went from Rome to France.

Antica, the ancient road, connecting the little Church of St. Mary of the Angels with Foligno. From there he was just a few minutes from his family property.

On the one hand, Francis previously loved seeing the new clothes and vibrant colors. On the other hand, he loathed the trip because the route would take him by the leper hospital of San Lazzaro[2] in the area of Arce.[3] Francis, like virtually everyone else in his day, hated being near the lepers. He was repulsed by their emaciated and pus-filled faces; their hideous, bloodshot eyes; and their awful stench. They were like walking ghosts with their hooded gray tunics.

Francis' father always said that lepers' thoughts were filthier than their bodies. He often told his son that they were filled with grudges and would avenge themselves on the townspeople who had cast them out at their first chance. Yet Francis

---

2 Virtually all leper hospital churches were dedicated to San Lazzaro (St. Lazarus)—the biblical beggar covered with sores—in the Middle Ages. In the fourteenth century, the name changed to St. Mary Magdalene. At that time, she was believed to have committed and been contaminated by every sexual sin until Jesus took her in and cleansed her from her stains.

3 In Francis' era, there were several other leprosaria (leper hospitals) in the valley below Assisi, though I focus mainly on the hospital of Arce, as it was the main one. San Salvatore delle Pareti was located on the main road from St. Mary of the Angels to Assisi. Today in its place stands a recently restored building, Villa Gualdo. The main leprosarium, however, was dedicated to San Lazarus and was in the vicinity of two chapels today known as Santa Maria Maddalena and San Rufino d'Arce. They are located between Rivotorto and the Portiuncula, adjacent to the St. Mary of the Angels Cemetery. Both churches remain well preserved today: San Rufino d'Arce is enclosed within the fenced property of the Franciscan Missionary Sisters of Susa; Santa Maria Maddalena is on the property of a family on a sharp bend in the road near the highway overpass.

was conflicted: even though he could not stand being in their presence, he had always felt a sense of pity for their plight.

Known today as Hansen's disease, leprosy is a disease of the peripheral nerves and mucosa of the upper respiratory tract caused by a particular bacterium. It is transmitted via droplets from the nose and mouth during close and frequent contact with infected people. If untreated, leprosy causes progressive and permanent damage to the skin, nerves, limbs, and eyes.

But the people of Francis' day did not understand things in a modern and scientific way. They did not consider leprosy merely a physical illness. No, it was considered a sign of God's disfavor—it was a curse.

Medieval people believed that only a thin veil separated the supernatural world from the natural world and that events and movements from one side easily interpenetrated the other. They believed that one reaped what he sowed (cf. Gal 6:7). Blessings followed good deeds and were from God, while bad things came from demons and were given to those who were not in favor with God.

In other words, they believed that those who had leprosy deserved it because of something they (or someone close to them) had done to merit God's disfavor. Thus the people shunned the lepers to avoid contamination—in both the physical and the spiritual sense.

As Francis passed by the hospital of San Lazzaro, he recalled the ancient Arthurian tale of Tristan and Isolde told by the French and Provençal troubadours who sometimes passed through Assisi:

> When King Mark learned of the adultery that his wife, Isolde, had committed with his lieutenant, Tristan, he decreed to

have her burned alive as punishment. Then, one hundred
lepers arrived with the sound of the clappers; their hands were
devoured by their disease, their faces splotched with whitish
stains, their eyes bloodshot. As they approached the fire, their
evil moved them to love the sight. And their chief, Ivan—the
ugliest of them all—cried out to the king, "Instead of the fire,
give her to your lepers. Then she will forever ask for death."

The king thought for a moment and consented, "Yes, she
shall live that life. For it is better justice and more terrible than
the flames."

And the lepers responded with glee, "Yes, throw her to
us, and make her one of us. Never shall a lady have known a
worse fate. Look at our rags and our abominations. Though
she has hitherto known only pleasure in wealth and fine
things, when she sees us, O King, with our filthy ways and
poor huts, then she will know the wrong she has done."

Then the hundred bestial lepers—filthy, screaming, and
shouting—pressed around her as she screamed in horror.

However, just then, Tristan arrived mounted on horseback.
He easily spurred and scattered the brutes and brought the
queen, his lover, to safety.[4]

Francis shuddered as he thought of the hideousness of the
lepers and spurred his horse to a gallop. Fortunately, there
were no lepers outside the hospital gates of the leprosarium
of Arce as he rode by and safely cleared the environs. Francis began to feel relieved and more settled as he approached
the area of Rivotorto.

His thoughts then turned toward a friend whom Francis
had known since childhood. Only a few months earlier, his
friend was discovered to have leprosy. Initially, the friend
tried to close himself off within his house and hide the fact

---

4 The story is adapted from M. Joseph Bédier, *The Romance of
Tristan and Iseult*, trans. H. Belloc (Edinburgh: Ballantyne, 1913),
http://www.gutenberg.org/files/14244/14244-h/14244-htm.

that he was infected. However, people soon began to wonder what had happened to him, and the doctors were called. Upon examination, they discovered leprous sores on his arms.

At once, his friend was taken from his house and brought to the Church of San Giorgio for the sending-off liturgy celebrated by the priest that would mark the man's separation from society. Francis was present in the church and he recalled very clearly the words of the priest during the ritual that would proclaim the man's permanent separation from the city of Assisi—from the world of the living to that of the living dead. As Francis' friend sat still, his relatives wept as if it were his funeral.

As the ecclesiastical statutes prescribed, the priest gave Francis' friend the gloomy tunic he would wear for the rest of his life—gray, full, and long.[5] He was given a little flask to drink from, a bowl to eat out of, and the ominous clapper. He was prohibited from drinking from wells or washing in local rivers and springs.

He was required to wear gloves and was forbidden to touch anything that was not his with his bare hands. He was further forbidden to speak with or be in the presence of any woman who was not a relative. He was forbidden from entering churches or from going to fairs, mills, or markets.

Touching children, or using public drinking cups or plates, was especially forbidden. Whenever he was in the presence of anyone, he was required to sound the clapper to warn others that he was close. He was even required to walk

---

5 Arnaldo Fortini describes the treatment of lepers in Assisi at length in *Francis of Assisi: A Translation of Nova Vita de San Francesco by Helen Moak* (New York: Crossroad, 1981), 206–10.

on a particular side of the road depending on the direction of the wind. Finally, the priest sprinkled earth on his head, signifying he was buried from the world.

A procession then formed to accompany Francis' friend down to the hospital of San Lazzaro near Arce, the one Francis had just passed. It consisted of the cross-bearer, the clerics, the priest, the leper, the man's family members, and a few faithful friends—including Francis. When they approached the Arce hospital, only the clerics and the leper were allowed onto the property.

By then, however, most of the man's friends and family had already said their permanent good-byes. Francis remained as long as possible and was able to look on in horror to see his friend's final dwelling place: a small cell with a wooden cross on the door. Inside were a meager bed, a table, a chair, and an oil lamp.

And that was it. It was over for his friend, who was now dead to the world. Francis' friend would live the remainder of his life in the hospital outside the city walls down in the valley with the other people who were just as disgraced as he was. For the rest of his life, by law, every time he was outside of the hospital and he came into contact with someone "pure," he would have to sound the clapper and yell "Unclean, unclean!" to alert them of his presence.

The city statutes dealing with leprosy were even harsher than the ecclesiastical ones. Just the year before, a new *podestà* (mayor) had gone through the city and countryside, as the statutes prescribed, searching for lepers. When some were found, they were beaten before being sent to the leper hospital.

Only once, when Francis was a child, had he seen a leper attempt to enter the city walls. The poor man was brutally beaten like a wild beast. Yet the offenders were not punished; in fact, the city's statutes protected anyone who beat a leper with impunity.

The custom of separating lepers from the community, however, went back much further than medieval times. It went all the way back to the Old Testament. The book of Leviticus dealt with extensive Jewish legislation regarding the diagnosis of leprosy and the person's consequential declaration of "clean" or "unclean." When a person was declared "unclean," they were separated from the community; if they were eventually healed and declared "clean," they could be reintegrated back into the community:

> The Lord said to Moses and Aaron: When someone has on the skin a mark, lesion, or blotch which appears to develop into a scaly infection, the person shall be brought to Aaron, the priest, or to one of the priests among his sons. If the priest, upon examination of the skin's infection, finds that the hair on the infection has turned white and the infection itself appears to be deeper than the skin, it is indeed a scaly infection; the priest, on seeing this, shall declare the person unclean. . . . As long as the infection is present, the person shall be unclean. Being unclean, that individual shall dwell apart, taking up residence outside the camp. (See Lv 13:1–3, 46.)

As Francis continued riding toward his family property, he tried to turn his thoughts to anything but the lepers. Once at the dye house, he focused on his work. When he finished, he set back to Assisi. However, something was about to happen that would change Francis' life forever.

As he rode by the area of Arce, Francis' horse noticed it first. It slowed from a trot to a walk, flattening its ears to alert and protect Francis. Only then did Francis hear the sound of that dreadful clapper: "Tah-ta-ta-ta-ta-ta-ta-ta-ta," followed by the raspy and strained voice: "Unclean . . . unclean." On the side of the road in the distance was a leper![6]

The sight of splotchy skin under that ominous, patched tunic made Francis shudder. Francis pulled back on his horse's reins and stopped. His initial reaction was to double back and take the longer route into Assisi. But even though every fiber within Francis' body screamed at him to get away from the leper, something within would not allow him. He could not turn away this time.

Francis remained still and watched the leper safely at a distance. His swollen face, disfigured body, and torn garments reminded Francis of Jesus on the cross. Francis had been spending a lot of time reflecting on how Jesus had reduced himself to the lowliest position—to the cross—out of great love. He recalled Scripture: "He was spurned and avoided by men, a man of suffering, knowing pain, Like one from whom you turn your face, spurned, and we held him in no esteem" (Is 53:3 NABRE).

Francis looked directly into the leper's bloodshot eyes. He saw a man imprisoned by pain, exclusion, and fear. Francis was now keenly aware of his own inner suffering. He considered how he had been held captive in the Perugia dungeon and had been mistreated by the cruel guards.

---

6 All the early sources refer to this encounter with the leper.

Francis had been released, but this man would surely die out there, alone, away from his family.

Francis, too, was feeling that pang of exclusion from family and old friends who no longer understood him after his return from Spoleto. He was discovering a sense of solidarity with the marginalized that were down in the valley. At that moment, Francis understood something of that horrible loneliness Jesus must have felt while hanging on the cross on Golgotha outside the city walls of Jerusalem, virtually alone, as most of his disciples had fled. He then began to understand Jesus' feelings of abandonment even by his own Father in heaven as he cried out from the cross, "My God, my God, why have you forsaken me?" (Mt 27:46 NABRE).

Francis saw clearly that the man standing in front of him was not really any different from himself; they shared a common experience, story, and humanity. They both had hurts, fears, and hopes. They were both good and beautifully created in the image of God.

Yet they were also both broken. Francis was now keenly aware of how disobedient he had been to God—how pride, envy, and vanity had controlled his life until a short time earlier. His sins now made him blush with shame.

Because of the brokenness that Francis carried within, he could relate to this man's disfigurement on the outside. Unlike some of the townspeople, however, Francis no longer believed that this man was being punished with leprosy as a consequence of sins—for even the innocent suffered. Rather, Francis began to view leprosy as a sign of the fallen condition of man.

Francis could no longer turn away. He had to do something that just a short time before would have been inconceivable. Trembling, Francis descended from his horse.

He approached the sick man with leprosy and embraced him. Then Francis genuflected before the man and kissed his face and deformed hands. The contrast between Francis—still dressed in fine garments—and the hideous leper in a tattered tunic was striking.

Up close, the man's face was horribly disfigured, the smell powerful, but the Holy Spirit jolted Francis with an energy and enthusiasm he had never felt before. This new vigor filled Francis with compassion that allowed him to look beyond the man's wretched condition and connect with his heart. In place of the stench, he smelled sweetness; instead of ugliness, he saw beauty. Francis recognized that the man's physical disease was no worse than the spiritual leprosy he carried within; on the contrary, Francis considered himself the greater sinner.

The man was no longer "a leper" to Francis—a creature with no name. Instead, he saw him as a human being, a person. Francis saw tears emerge from the man's blood-shot eyes.

After so much suffering, sickness, and exile, the man had succumbed to the belief that he was truly wretched and undeserving of love. At some point, he had believed the lie that he was indeed cursed, abandoned by God, and that he deserved his illness as a punishment for something he had done, some sin his parents had committed, or that God never loved him from the outset. Yet the embrace of this well-dressed, saintly man restored a sense of dignity within him, and he realized he was not a monster or an outcast, but he was indeed loved.

In that embrace, both Francis and the man experienced healing. In that moment, the bitterness within Francis—and the leper—was transformed into sweetness. Everything Francis had loved carnally and desired to have he now despised and hated; what before had seemed delightful and sweet had become unbearable and bitter; and what before made him shudder now offered him great sweetness and enormous delight.[7]

In Francis' encounter with the lepers, he was modeling his Savior who had once said, "Take my yoke upon you, and learn from me; for I am gentle and lowly in heart" (Mt 11:29). No longer could Francis relate to the leper according to the ancient custom of Levitican legislation—separation from the community. Now he was acting like Christ: "And a leper came to him beseeching him, and kneeling said to him, 'If you will, you can make me clean.' Moved with pity, he stretched out his hand and touched him, and said to him, 'I will; be clean.' And immediately the leprosy left him, and he was made clean. And he sternly charged him, and sent him away at once, and said to him, 'See that you say nothing to any one; but go, show yourself to the priest, and offer for your cleansing what Moses commanded, for a proof to the people'" (Mk 1:40–44).

The leper approached Jesus crying not "Unclean" but "If you will, you can make me clean." Jesus responded with pity and compassion, reached out, touched the sick man,

---

7 See "The Legend of the Three Companions," in *Francis of Assisi: Early Documents*, ed. and trans. Regis J. Armstrong, vol. 2, *The Founder* (Hyde Park, NY: New City Press, 2000), chap. 4, 11.

and healed him from leprosy. In being cleansed, the leper was able to return to the priest to be declared "clean" so that he could become reintegrated within the community. The effects of Christ's healing were not only freedom from the physical plight of leprosy but reinstatement within the community through an end to banishment and social marginalization.

In Francis' encounter with the leper, the man was probably not cured from the physical disease of leprosy and he would not return to his former community within the city gates of Assisi. However, in a spiritual sense, the man was reintegrated within the community of believers. He now had faith and confidence that he was not separated from God and that one day he would be fully united with the Father in the kingdom of heaven.

In that embrace, Francis understood that the merchants, bankers, and artisans of Assisi were not the true Minors—those with the disease of leprosy were. The lepers were the lowliest in medieval society. And now, because of his contact with them, so was Francis. But perhaps Christ was the most "minor" of them all, since it was he—the Son of God—who had humbled himself the most by separating himself from his own Father and emptying himself of the glories of heaven to assume the human condition down to its lowliest, most wretched part: the cross.

"Surely he has borne our griefs and carried our sorrows; yet we esteemed him stricken, smitten by God, and afflicted. But he was wounded for our transgressions, he was bruised for our iniquities; upon him was the chastisement that made us whole, and with his stripes we are healed" (Is 53:4–5). Jesus' death on the cross was God's connection with all sin, suffering, and alienation, which he assumed onto himself. The kingdom of heaven would seep down to the lowliest parts of creation—all the way down to the leper.

And it was precisely from the poverty of his cross that Jesus was resurrected by the work of the Trinity. The cross was not the final condition, the Resurrection was! Indeed, while hanging on the cross, Jesus had expressed feelings of abandonment by his own Father in heaven, while in fact he was reciting Psalm 22, which begins with the Psalmist's desolation and feelings of abandonment and concludes with his praising God in consolation!

Despite hanging on the cross, Jesus had the faith and hope that he would soon be raised from the cross. Evil never triumphs over good! The cross and Resurrection, death and life, were inseparably intertwined; yet life always prevailed.

The Resurrection was the victory of faith that gave meaning and hope to all suffering. And through Jesus' resurrection, both Francis and the man with leprosy were elevated from their own suffering human condition. Because of the poverty of God, they could praise God and share in the glories of heaven even though they were not yet there: "Though he was rich, yet for your sake he became poor, so that by his poverty you might become rich" (2 Cor 8:9).

Toward the end of his life, Francis would write in his *Testament* that this encounter with the man with leprosy marked the beginning of his penance—his conversion: "The Lord granted me, Brother Francis, to begin to do penance in this way: While I was in sin, it seemed very bitter to me to see lepers. And the Lord himself led me among them and I had mercy upon them. And when I left them that which seemed bitter to me was changed into sweetness of soul and body; and afterward I lingered a little and left the world."[8]

In reality, however, Francis' penance had already begun, and his soul had been prepared to respond to this moment of grace through his failure at attaining knighthood, his imprisonment in the Perugian dungeon, the voice in Spoleto that asked whether it was better to serve the servant or the master, that peculiar illness that would not allow him to find joy in his old amusements, his long periods of prayer in solitary places, his encounter with the cross.

The embrace with the leper was, in actuality, not the beginning of his penance but rather the *culmination* of his penance. It was the moment in which he learned to relate to God, to others, and to himself as Jesus did. As a minor. Not like the Assisi Minors—who were constantly obsessed with commercial gain and political expansion—but like the true minor who came for the humble and the oppressed: Jesus, the Christ.

Francis would work with the lepers around Assisi for the rest of his life. However, he never encountered that same man again.

---

8 St. Francis, "The Testament," in *Francis and Clare: The Complete Works*, trans. Regis J. Armstrong (Mahwah, NJ: Paulist Press, 1982), 1–3.

6

THE CRUCIFIX SPEAKS

Now we have received not the spirit of the world, but the Spirit which is from God, that we might understand the gifts bestowed on us by God.

1 CORINTHIANS 2:12

F RANCIS' penances became more and more intense. He began withdrawing more and more to caves and isolated places outside of Assisi for prayer and reflection.

Francis had always been generous, but now his largesse took on religious meaning. He gave away money, clothes, and food to the poor. He bought furnishings for churches. He went on pilgrimage to Rome, to the threshold of Sts. Peter and Paul, as Rome was referred to then. There he was struck by the number of beggars, and he traded clothes with one of them.

In this, he not only identified with them but started becoming one of them.[1] Before returning to Assisi, he took a large handful of coins and threw them on the tomb of St. Peter. He believed the other pilgrims were giving

---

1 Cf. Bonaventure of Bagnoregio, "The Major Legend of Saint Francis," in *Francis of Assisi: Early Documents*, ed. and trans. Regis J. Armstrong, vol. 2, *The Founder* (Hyde Park, NY: New City Press, 2000), chap. 1, 6.

6

grudgingly and miserly. In all this, Francis was experiencing a conversion. He was turning away from one way of life and embracing another.

Francis was embracing the life of the lay-penitents who lived around and passed through Assisi. The penitents had been around for centuries. They were mostly laypersons not under an established religious Rule or monastery.

They lived alone or in small communities, as hermits in the hills, or as recluses in their homes. Sometimes they lived near a church or monastery and prayed together with the community as an oblate or *conversus*, but they never professed a formal Rule. They were single or married, consecrated or lay, men or women. They fasted often and prayed daily, they wore penitential tunics, they refrained from military service and avoided professions as merchants or public servants.

Francis' penances included physical asceticism. Asceticism seemed to Francis the best way to counter his inordinate desire for pleasure and comfort and his natural tendencies, which were inclined toward selfishness and self-centeredness. He began wearing a hair shirt (the rough wool or horsehair garment worn directly against the skin under the garments), fasting, and engaging in other corporal disciplines. Sometimes Francis' corporal penances were severe and his disciplines were strict.

Francis often referred to his body as "Brother Donkey," whose stubbornness he felt necessary to deal with harshly.[2] He ate little, and when he did, he mixed his food with ashes

---

2 Cf. Thomas of Celano, "The Remembrance of the Desire of a Soul," in *Francis of Assisi: Early Documents*, vol. 2, *The Founder*, chap. 92.

or bitter herbs to kill the taste. He slept rarely, often using stones as pillows. He responded to temptation by disrobing and rolling around in the snow or in thorn bushes.

Francis was harsh on his body because he believed that sin dwelt there within. He would later write, "Many people, when they sin or receive an injury, often blame the Enemy or a neighbor, but this is not right, for each one has the real enemy in his own power; that is, the body through which he sins."[3] Yet when referring to the body, he really meant the flesh: "But I say, walk by the Spirit, and do not gratify the desires of the flesh. For the desires of the flesh are against the Spirit, and the desires of the Spirit are against the flesh; for these are opposed to each other" (Gal 5:16–17).

Francis believed that the body was good, yet sin resided within its flesh, which he was seeking to discipline—even quell—through his corporal penances. He never believed the body was bad, as did the Cathars. Rather, through self-mortifications, he was seeking to detach himself from the desires of the flesh and the pleasures of the world.[4]

For Francis, penance was biblical; it meant "conversion."[5] In his penance, Francis turned from sin and had a change

---

3 St. Francis, "The Admonitions," in *Francis and Clare: The Complete Works*, trans. Regis J. Armstrong (Mahwah, NJ: Paulist Press, 1982), chap. 10.

4 The Cathars were a sect originating in the East, whose dualistic beliefs echoed those of fifth-century Manichaeism. Also known as Albigensians from Albi, France, they believed in two gods: the good god of the spirit and the bad god of matter. Like the mendicant orders, they embraced poverty; however, they did so because they rejected the world as evil.

5 A wonderful book describing the history of this movement in the Church and in the origins of the Franciscan movement is Raffaele Pazzelli, *St. Francis and the Third Order* (Chicago: Franciscan Herald Press, 1989). Pazzelli notes that the origins of the practice of penance are found

of heart. In his penance, he was allowing his body to become a living sacrifice (cf. Rm 12:1). In his flesh, he was completing what is lacking in Christ's afflictions (cf. Col 1:24). He had picked up his cross and was following Jesus (cf. Mk 8:34).

For Francis, the most perfect way to live penance—and conversion—was by serving people with leprosy. Francis returned again and again to serve the lepers near the hospital of Arce. He stayed with them and served all of them with great love. He talked to them and spent time with them. He also washed and cleaned the pus from their sores.[6]

The leper was the antithesis of Francis' former life. This was his radical conversion: Just a little while earlier, Francis had wanted to become a knight and associate with the greatest people. Now, after meeting Jesus Christ, he wanted to associate with the least.

The lepers provided the most concrete way of living the gospel for Francis. In his encounter with them, he demonstrated that penance was not merely an external action or a corporal discipline but a change of heart, a *metanoia*. Through his embrace of the leper, Francis' bitterness was changed into sweetness, and he was transformed. Thus

---

in the Bible. In the original Greek New Testament, both Jesus and John the Baptist urge their followers toward *metanoia*, which means "change of heart." In the Gospel of Matthew they say "*Metanoeite!*" which was later translated into the Latin Vulgate as "*Agite poenitentiam!*" (literally, "do penance") and then into English as "Repent, the kingdom is at hand!" Thus the original biblical meaning of penance is to repent, or to have a change of heart and turn from sin.

6 See Thomas of Celano, "The Life of Saint Francis," in *Francis of Assisi: Early Documents*, ed. and trans. Regis J. Armstrong, vol. 1, *The Saint* (Hyde Park, NY: New City Press, 1999), chap. 7, 17.

penance for Francis was always accompanied by an *internal* change of heart.

Francis now had a new enthusiasm and a consolation he had never before felt. Even when he was excited about becoming a knight, it had never totally satisfied his heart. That desire, although heartfelt, had always left him feeling restless, sometimes even irritable. But now he knew that something was different: he was wholeheartedly engaged in a new direction and a new mission.

He had been transformed. From now on, he would seek to imitate Jesus in everything. He would embrace the cross and seek only humility. His path was clear; the cross and Scriptures were his guides. Francis became minor by serving lepers, renouncing worldly privileges, giving away possessions, and dying to himself. He was imitating Jesus.

One day while returning to Assisi near the Church of San Damiano, Francis felt an unusually strong longing to go inside. He felt a desire to place himself before the crucifix. He entered the church and knelt in front of the altar facing the East—the Orient—the direction of the Holy Land and the rising morning light.

Francis spent a lot of time gazing at the crucifix of San Damiano. The cross was the only theology Francis would ever have his entire life. He would never need to delve into the weighty theological issues of the day expounded upon in Latin in the universities and theologates throughout Europe. The cross taught him everything.

He gazed deeply into the crucifix, and its rich symbolism continued to speak to him. Whereas initially Francis could only see Jesus' suffering, now he began to see beyond Christ's suffering. He noticed how the black color in the background, the symbol of death, was dominated by the light of Jesus, the symbol of life. He recalled Scripture: "I am the light of the world; he who follows me will not walk in darkness, but will have the light of life" (Jn 8:12).

Other colors like red—the symbol of love—stood out, while the entire icon was hemmed in by gold, the symbol of eternal glory. Francis recognized the scallop shells that outlined the entire cross; he was familiar with the shell on the tunics of pilgrims who made their way to the tomb of St. James in Compostela, Spain. The scallop was a Christian symbol of eternal life: the mollusk dies, as does the human body, but the shell lives forever, like the soul.

Francis then considered how Jesus was standing upright without any sign of relaxation in his arms and legs. He was alive, not dead! His arms were wide open and slightly flexed, demonstrating a total offering and openness toward God and humanity. He was embracing those who followed him to the cross—Mary his mother, John, Mary of Magdala, and Mary, the mother of James. Yet his embrace encompassed the lesser figures as well, like the soldiers— Stephen, the Centurion, and Longinus, the Roman soldier who pierced Jesus' side with a lance.

Finally, above Jesus, the right hand of God the Father offered a blessing. Through the crucifix, Francis began to become aware of God's total love for humanity through Jesus' incarnation, suffering, death, resurrection, ascension, and glory. "For God so loved the world that he gave his only Son, that whoever believes in him should not perish but have eternal life" (Jn 3:16). Jesus Christ saves!

After a long period of prayer, Francis felt an overpowering presence of the love of God deep within his heart. It was almost as if the Lord had emerged from the crucifix itself and entered directly into Francis' heart, so powerful was his awareness of God. He became profoundly aware of his own sinfulness and weakness, but he was deeply consoled because he felt God's great love abound.

In fact, God was present in Francis' heart precisely because of his awareness of his own weakness and sinfulness. He sensed the awesome power of the Holy Spirit—that he can move mountains (cf. Mt 17:20). Francis' heart was exhilarated. He asked only one question: "Lord, what do you want me to do?"

Then he heard the voice. This was the third time he heard it: "Francis, go and rebuild my house, which, as you can see, is totally in ruin." The voice then repeated itself two more times.[7]

It made perfect sense. He would set about repairing San Damiano. He had entered that ruined church a short time before as a broken man, but he had been restored there in the church. His own house had been rebuilt.

Even though Francis still thought of himself as a weak, sinful man, he had a new strength, a new power. For the Holy Spirit was now working within him. Inside that little church dedicated to the two saintly physician brothers,

---

7 The encounter with Christ in front of the crucifix was a key moment in Francis' life, referred to by all the sources. See Bonaventure, "Major Legend," chap. 2, 1; Celano, "The Remembrance," 10; and "The Legend of the Three Companions," in *Francis of Assisi: Early Documents*, vol. 2, *The Founder*, 13. Only the Bonaventure source says the voice spoke three times; the others refer to just once.

the Holy Spirit healed him and gave him new life. Now Francis would set about repairing the Church of San Damiano and bring it, too, back to life. Many more souls would be healed there.

Francis now clearly understood the question the Lord had posed to him that night in Spoleto. He now realized how he had been serving servants his entire life. Until then, Francis had never sought to serve the true Lord. He had always been distracted by worldly lords and what they could do for him or give him—his father, the nobility, knights, military commanders, even the pope.[8] But, perhaps more than all, he had been serving himself and his own desires and goals.

He finally understood that he had been trying to appropriate to himself what was not his to take. That was the true war that raged within his soul. He had been willing to kill in exchange for earthly glory. Now he sought with his entire being to surrender his will to God. The following prayer flowed from his heart and mind: "Most High glorious God, enlighten the darkness of my heart and give me, Lord, a correct faith, a certain hope, a perfect charity, sense and knowledge, so that I may carry out your holy and true command. Amen."[9]

He set out to follow the Lord's command with no misunderstanding. At that moment, Francis was to rebuild the

---

8 During the Middle Ages, popes were not only spiritual leaders of the Catholic Church; they were temporal lords who ruled over much of central Italy. In fact, when Francis sought out knighthood the second time (when he turned back in Spoleto), he was attempting to fight for the pope in a crusade against the excommunicated emperor, Otto.

9 This prayer is mentioned in several manuscripts. They all indicate that Francis prayed it at the foot of the crucifix of San Damiano.

particular Church of San Damiano. He was given a precise instruction that he was to accomplish then. The command to rebuild that particular church would expand to other churches around Assisi. He would later rebuild San Pietro of Spina and St. Mary of the Angels in the valley.

Yet the broken-down churches symbolized the ruinous condition of the greater Church. And in fact, his command to "rebuild God's house" would eventually grow and develop into a mission to rebuild the universal Church. But for now, Francis was doing just what God asked of him. And he would spend the remainder of his life consciously or unconsciously responding to the command he received in San Damiano.

When Francis received the command to rebuild the Lord's house, the crucifix at San Damiano was imprinted interiorly within his soul. The marks would remain a secret between Francis and God. Although Francis would never boast about having the secret stigmata within, he would remain devoted to the cross and would always recall it in everything. The marks of the cross would remain between Francis and God for the next twenty years until Laverna, when they would be finally exposed on his body. Then he could say, like Paul, "I bear on my body the marks of Jesus" (Gal 6:17).

Francis was impetuous. It was a trait that would prompt him to do great things in his life—both worldly and spiritual—but at times would make him foolish. He had often taken money from his father's shop for feasts and extravagant things, and his father never really seemed to mind. So without serious reflection, he promptly went to the family warehouse and took a bolt of fine cloth.

Then he went to the stable and saddled one of the horses. He rode fifteen miles to the Foligno marketplace, where he sold the cloth and the horse to the first buyer. Now he had money and could begin rebuilding the ruined Church of San Damiano.

Francis returned to Assisi several hours later on foot. Even though the priest at San Damiano was not very educated, he was wise. Francis thought the priest would be enthusiastic to have money to begin repairing the church. Instead, he reacted cautiously and refused to accept the money.

The priest knew of Pietro's temperament and of Francis' strained relationship with him. Francis was disappointed, and he tossed the moneybag onto a window in the church.[10] He suddenly had an intuition that he had done something wrong. Terribly wrong. He went to be alone to think things through. He nervously began to ask himself if he should have taken and sold the cloth.

---

10 The window, now closed, can still be seen in the Church of San Damiano. It is known locally as the "money window."

7

SPIRITUAL SWORD

Do not think that I have come to bring peace on earth; I have not come to bring peace, but a sword. For I have come to set a man against his father, and a daughter against her mother, and a daughter-in-law against her mother-in-law; and a man's foes will be those of his own household.

MATTHEW 10:34–36

PIETRO returned home after a long business journey. He was exhausted, dirty, and hungry. Before greeting him at the door, Pietro's servant closed his eyes, took a deep breath, and said, "Francis is not here. He hasn't been home in weeks."

"Where is my son?" Pietro roared.

His servant stammered, "He is going through town asking people to help him rebuild a dilapidated country church outside the walls. He took an expensive bolt of cloth from your warehouse and sold it along with one of your finest horses. We don't know where he is, although we have reports that he is actually living with the lepers."

The servant braced for Pietro's reaction. Pietro remained still and began to tremble. His color went red and he clenched his fists.

He carefully instructed the servant to bring Francis to him. Without saying another word, Pietro's servant nodded and backed out of the room. He kept his head down, but he cautiously fixed his eyes on Pietro's hands.

Pietro's servants found Francis at the leper hospital. They brought him to his father, who beat him and chained him in the cellar of the family home.[1] Communal statutes gave a father the right to imprison a son who had squandered family assets within the family house.

Pietro was forced to leave again on business. However, while he was away, Francis' mother, Pica, had mercy on her son and set him free. Francis then hid in a cave near San Damiano to consider his father's reaction.

Initially, selling the cloth seemed like the right thing to do. The voice—God—told him to rebuild the church. But when the priest would not accept the money, Francis knew he had made a mistake.

So many things had happened in the past few years between him and his father. In fact, Francis had actually been impressed by his father's patience. Now, however, he feared that the cloth would be the last straw.

Francis was the firstborn son. In the Middle Ages, this meant that his father's possessions would be Francis' due inheritance through his right of primogeniture. His younger brother, Angelo, Pietro's second-born son, did not have that right. It was Francis who was destined to succeed his father as *paterfamilias* who would continue the family name and

---

1 In the church of Chiesa Nuova, a small cell commemorates Francis' imprisonment by his father.

tradition. To remain in the family meant maintaining the family line.

Francis was anxious again. He felt like his conversion was being tested. The reality of his situation began to set in. Up until that moment, Francis had his feet in both worlds. Pietro had always supported him and his endeavors, and Francis had always relied on his father's security, resources, servants, and money. Never before had he been forced to provide for himself on his own.

Would he be able to get by? How? What would he do? He began to question his new life.

Francis resorted to what he had been learning at San Damiano: prayer. Prayer had become his new strength. After a long period of deep prayer, Francis became conscious of God's total and deep love for him.

Slowly, joy and sweetness began to flood into his soul. His anxiety began to fade, and the doubts and fears of the things of the world began to leave him. He was filled with an inner conviction that God loved him and that his grace was at work within him. His desolation was transformed into consolation.

Francis was now dedicated to following the minor Christ. He had a choice: Christ or the ways of the world, spiritual prince or worldly prince.

His father would never accept Francis' new way of life, nor would he allow him to continue in it if he had any control. A life that began in wealth but chose minority and humility was the opposite of his father's life experience, who had been born poor and became rich. There was no way he would ever understand how his son, born rich, could choose to become poor. Francis understood that he had to choose one world or the other. He knew what to do.

When Pietro returned home and discovered his son missing again, he was infuriated. He was angry at his son for his disobedience and misguided ways, at his wife for letting Francis go, at the priest for leading his "oblate" in mischief, at the townspeople who believed Pietro was like his son. He knew he had to do it; it was long overdue.

His firstborn son had brought shame and dishonor to his family. He considered Francis a spendthrift who did not recognize the value of money. He believed his son was a coward for turning back from battle in Spoleto. Francis hemmed and hawed on his life's direction. And now his own son had stolen from him!

Perhaps the worst thing, however, was that he was actually living with lepers! Everyone knew Francis was a bit eccentric, but his actions were now erratic and intolerable. Pietro had witnessed plenty of those fanatic "penitents" wandering around preaching penitence and religion, but when no one was looking, they would steal and lie. And now his firstborn son was one of them.

Francis had become a liability to the family. In order for the tree to continue to grow, he had to cut off the diseased limb. If he did not, people would judge Pietro to be as crazy as his son.

It was customary then to call together a "council" consisting of relatives and neighbors to help decide what to do. Pietro's relatives agreed with him: Francis was a rebellious squanderer. This was not good for Francis, since the city statues dealt harshly with the "squandering and rebellion" of a son: "The son who does not give obedience to his father and to his mother, at their request is to be banished from the city and from the district, and no one may give him anything to eat or to drink or help him in any way."[2]

However, now there was the thorny issue that Francis was claiming to be a penitent and an oblate of the Church of San Damiano. Therefore, he was not under the jurisdiction of the consuls of the commune; rather, he was under the protection of the Church. So Francis' father would have to go to the head of the Church in Assisi, Bishop Guido, to demand reparations, since his son—now a "son" of the Church—had stolen from him. The bishop agreed to hear the case, and he summoned Francis and Pietro to his residence, known as the *vescovado*, next to the former cathedral church of Assisi, Santa Maria Maggiore.[3]

Bishop Guido was a powerful man. He was accustomed to conflict and had spent plenty of time in the tribunals defending his own diocesan property and privileges. Even though he was used to mediation, he was not happy to

---

2 Arnaldo Fortini, *Francis of Assisi: A Translation of Nova Vita de San Francesco by Helen Moak* (New York: Crossroad, 1981), 224–25.

3 The Church of Santa Maria Maggiore was the seat of the bishop (cathedral) of Assisi until the eleventh century when it was transferred to San Rufino. The bishop's residence, however, is still next to Santa Maria Maggiore. The present church was built over the ruins of an early Christian church of the fourth century, itself perhaps built over an ancient Roman noble palace. The interior was formerly decorated with frescoes that were destroyed during an earthquake in 1852. The separation between Francis and his father here marked the moment when Francis definitively broke from the stability and security of his old life, choosing to embrace a life of penance and poverty dedicated to the poor, crucified Christ. It is not known whether Francis ever reconciled with his father. After his conversion, his family members are no longer mentioned in the thirteenth-century sources. It is believed that Pietro died shortly afterwards.

witness a father and son, two spiritual sons of his, in such a situation. He wished to be neutral, although religion was at the center of the conflict.

Francis came voluntarily. He carried a conviction in his heart that he was following and imitating Christ alone. He knew he could not serve two masters—he would hate one and love the other (cf. Mt 6:24). Francis was perhaps the only person who knew what the outcome of that audience would be.

The local townspeople watched in amazement as Francis, ashen and thin, entered through the Moiano gate dressed in shredded clothes. Some were horrified at his appearance; others were maliciously gleeful at the downfall of one of Assisi's most promising citizens. They jeered, "He's drunk too much bad wine! . . . He's crazy! . . . He's possessed by a demon! . . . Look at Assisi's most promising citizen now— the great prince!"

The children threw rocks and mud at him as they, too, insulted him. But Francis found consolation as he thought of Christ, who was also misunderstood by his townspeople: "Truly, I say to you, no prophet is acceptable in his own country" (Lk 4:24).

Francis arrived at the large piazza adjacent to the *vescovado* next to the Church of Santa Maria Maggiore. The square was spacious in order to accommodate the crowds that gathered regularly to receive blessings from the bishop, watch processions, or hear ecclesial trials. Today it was packed. News travels quickly in a small town, and the throngs were always excited to watch a fight.

Francis' father arrived surrounded with his retinue of relatives, neighbors, business cohorts, and public consuls.

He pushed his way toward the front of the crowd. The bishop came out of his residence dressed solemnly in his episcopal mitre and blue velvet mantle. He seated himself in his *cathedra*, or "throne," and, with the wave of his hand, commenced the *pro tribunali* audience.

Francis' father spoke first: "Your Excellency, my lord, I have loved my son as it is a father's duty. I raised him properly. I prepared him to become a great prince: I gave him everything he needed and much more; I paid for him to learn to read and write through the canons at your own episcopal school of San Giorgio; I taught him the trade of being a merchant, which he squandered; I paid for his training to be a knight and purchased the finest armor and war-horse on two separate occasions, which he squandered.

"As you well know, the second time he turned away from battle and came back to Assisi as a coward. In your own school, he learned about religion. The religion your clerics taught him was respectable, decent, and honorable. But look at him now!

"He's living with the lepers and claiming religion as his reason for doing so! He has made my family the laughing-stock of Assisi! And now he has stolen my best cloth and horse from me, which he sold to rebuild some dilapidated country church outside the walls! I will no longer allow him to remain in my family after having offended it so greatly. Do you see what he has done to me?"

Turning to Francis, Bishop Guido told him that stealing was wrong and against the commandments. He asked him to give back the money he stole. Francis knelt and addressed his father, though he was facing the crowd. With eyes closed, he proclaimed, "Pietro di Bernardone, I give you back what I took from you."

He then revealed the money bag that he had received in exchange for his father's cloth and horse. He tossed it on the ground in front of the bishop to the prelate's relief. But then Francis did something unexpected. He proceeded to remove his clothes, which he placed on top of the money.

With tears welling up in his eyes, he continued speaking. His voice quivered due to the cold as well as emotion. "Lord Bishop, I give back everything my earthly father has given me: not only the money he has given me but even the clothes he has given me. Until now I have called you, Pietro di Bernardone, my father, but from now on I have only one Father—our Father who art in heaven."

He had now removed all his clothes. He stood as a naked man following the naked Christ: "Nudam crucem nudus sequar" (Naked, I will follow the naked cross).

Francis opened his eyes to see his father's fist clenched and attempting to strike him, only to be blocked by a cohort who restrained him. Francis then looked up in the sky toward heaven and saw a vision. A heavenly hand protruded from the clouds with the index and middle fingers extended in the form of a traditional blessing.

At once, Francis was cursed by his earthly father but blessed by his heavenly Father.[4] Francis knew that he was listening to the voice of his true Father.

Bishop Guido quickly moved toward Francis, covered him with his mantle, and brought him into his palace. Not

---

4 This image is beautifully depicted in one of the Giotto frescoes in the Upper Basilica of St. Francis.

only did Francis have a new Father; he had a new Mother, as well—the Church. He would be protected, nurtured, and cared for in his new life.

The people were stunned and a hush came over the crowd. His father picked up his money, left the clothes, and departed, grumbling that he would not be made the fool in this. Bishop Guido was moved at what he had just witnessed. He considered the biblical verse: "Do not think that I have come to bring peace on earth; I have not come to bring peace, but a sword. For I have come to set a man against his father, and a daughter against her mother, and a daughter-in-law against her mother-in-law; and a man's foes will be those of his own household" (Mt 10:34–36).

Bishop Guido felt sad about the conflict but also joyful about Francis' newfound vocation. He wondered to himself if he would have been able to give up everything for the love of Christ as did this young, passionate man in front of him. He thought about all the castles and palaces he owned in Assisian territory—how he had fought in the tribunals to keep them and had issued anathemas and invectives against those who challenged him.

Francis received the blessing of the bishop and he left Assisi. He had now divested himself of the last trace of his worldly life. He was completely open to what his Father alone would provide even if he did not know where he was going.

8

GO FORTH: THROUGH CREATION TO GUBBIO

Go from your country and your kindred and your father's house to the land that I will show you.

GENESIS 12:1

FRANCIS left Bishop Guido's residence still covered in his episcopal mantle. As he passed through the streets of Assisi, he was trembling, and tears were streaming down his face. Some of the townspeople followed, heckling and taunting him.

Though his will was resolute, his heart was crushed. His parents had given him life. They had nursed him, cared for him, and loved him. Francis had been through some challenging ordeals in his life—arduous journeys, training for battle, imprisonment, and illness—but never had he done something as difficult as this.

Perhaps the saddest thing was that his father could not see the beauty of Francis' new life, which he considered worthless. He thought his son was a fanatic.

"What kind of prince have I become?" he asked himself. Francis felt a tremendous sadness and wondered if he would do great things yet. Or would he remain a failure as he was now?

Francis found a farmer's tunic near the episcopal court of Moiano, which he put on. He dressed like the penitents who worked with the lepers around Assisi and in Rome, with a rough wool tunic, leather belt, and boots. He found some chalk and drew a cross in the form of a tau on his tunic. The Greek letter *tau* is the equivalent of the Hebrew letter *taw*, the last letter of the Hebrew alphabet. Tau has the same form as the letter *T*.

For Francis, the tau would become the symbol of his penance, his conversion. He would use it in his writings, sign his name with it, and paint it on places where he stayed. The visible cross and tunic would declare him a man dedicated wholly to God and serve as an external sign of his interior conversion.[1]

As he walked through Assisi's narrow streets with high walls toward the San Giacomo gate, Francis looked around

---

1 Francis came into contact with the tau while caring for lepers in Assisi when he met the Antonians, a religious Order founded in 1095 to care for lepers that wore the letter on their tunics as a sign of penance. Pope Innocent III would refer to the tau in the book of Ezekiel upon opening the Fourth Lateran Council a few years later on November 11, 1215, in reference to laxity and corruption in the Church as well as the profaning of the Holy Land by the Saracens: "Then he called to the man dressed in linen with the writer's case at his waist, saying to him: 'Pass through the city (of Jerusalem) and mark an X (tau) on the foreheads of those who moan and groan over all the abominations that are practiced within it" (see Ez 9:3–4). The pope would say at the same council, "The tau has exactly the same form as the Cross on which our Lord was crucified on Calvary, and only those will be marked with this sign and will obtain mercy who have mortified their flesh and conformed their life to that of the Crucified Savior." Pope Innocent announced that for him, for the Church, and for every Catholic at the time, the symbol they were to take as the sign of their Passover was the tau cross. He ended his homily by saying, "Be champions of the tau."

at his native city, which he adored so dearly. It was always loud and bustling. Boisterous men went about singing or yelling at each other in loud arguments, while children played in the alleys.

The town herald and criers moved through the streets shouting out directives and events. Vendors hawked silk, wool, and velvet, while men bartered loudly with peddlers at their tables over oil and produce. Peasants led horses and donkeys pulling their carts, while chickens and pigs roamed about eating refuse off the streets. Women washed clothes in the wash fountains and gathered water from the wells and cisterns.

Francis took in the lovely aromas of bread baking and sauces simmering wafting from the women's kitchens. All the while, cripples and beggars went about asking for money. How he loved his native city and would miss it.

Yet Francis knew he had to leave Assisi. He would give his father the justice he sought and voluntarily exile himself. He was like Abram as he went forth from the land of his kinsfolk and from his father's house to receive a new life and a new name, Abraham (see Gn 12:1).

Francis, too, wondered if he should change his name. He was no longer Francis—the merchant of France, the wealthy prince, the great knight. He was now following in the footsteps of his baptismal namesake, John. He was now a penitent. Like Abraham, Francis was going forward to the land that God would show him, even if he had no idea where that land was.

No, Francis did not know where he was headed, but he believed he was going in the right direction. Even so, he still felt conflicted. It was clear now that he was not called to become a worldly prince, but was the prophecy true? Would he one day be great?

He also felt conflicted about leaving his father. Would he, like Abraham, eventually be blessed with numerous children and land? Was he following the commandment to honor his mother and father (see Ex 20:12)?

Scripture said that by honoring them, he would add years to his life.[2] If he was not honoring his father, would years be taken away from his life? Would he be cursed?

As he exited the San Giacomo gate, he walked a few hundred yards, then stopped and looked back at the city walls. He was now alone and in exile. More than just providing security, the walls offered a sense of community and citizenship, which he had now renounced.

Francis was now outside both the protection and the community of Assisi. Perhaps forever. Francis looked at the statues of Mary and St. Christopher above the gate. He would need their intercession, as he was now separated from his Assisi and her safety.

The roads were dangerous, as they were full of brigands and other armed men. There was also the threat of attacks by wolves, boars, or dogs. Francis would now be embracing a permanently precarious state of life.

As he walked down the hill behind Assisi known by locals as the Hill of Hell, he shuddered as he considered all the criminals who were executed there. Yet Francis had no way of knowing that in just twenty-five years, he

2 See Arnaldo Fortini, *Francis of Assisi: A Translation of Nova Vita de San Francesco by Helen Moak* (New York: Crossroad, 1981), 224–25.

would be buried there underneath a huge, modern basilica constructed in his honor, and because of him, the hill's name would be forever changed to the Hill of Paradise. He continued walking among the olive trees behind the Hill of Hell toward the monastery of Santa Maria degli Episcopi. Then he crossed the Galli Bridge over the Tescio River, full of gushing water from the heavy melting snows. He passed by the mill belonging to the monks of San Paolo, whose monastery was close to his father's home. From there, he continued on the old road between Assisi and Gubbio—the one that passed through Valfabbrica, where the ancient castle and feudal towers stood.

Indeed, as Francis reached the little country church of San Nicolo di Campolungo near the border between Assisi and Perugia, he was jumped by robbers. With Perugian accents, they demanded to know who he was and which lord he served. They were trying to decide whether to rob him.

Francis excitedly proclaimed that he was now in the service of the true Lord, and he shouted out, "I am the Herald of the Great King." They just laughed as they beat him and threw him in the snowbank. Bruised and battered, Francis brushed himself off and continued walking.

They did not take away his joy, and Francis praised the Creator in an ever-louder voice.[3] Francis handled his first tribulation well. He rejoiced that he had been found worthy so early in his new life to receive the same harsh treatment as his Lord. He continued walking.

---

3 See Bonaventure of Bagnoregio, "The Major Legend of Saint Francis," in *Francis of Assisi: Early Documents*, ed. and trans. Regis J. Armstrong, vol. 2, *The Founder* (Hyde Park, NY: New City Press, 2000), chap. 2, 5.

Francis had no plans or goals. He just walked and walked. He was accustomed to long caravan trips with his father; however, walking was very different from riding his horse. It was much more tiring.

His legs were well conditioned from constantly walking up and down the numerous staircases and steep gradations of Assisi, built as it was on the slopes of Mount Subasio. But walking through the mountains and hills was strenuous. Yet there was no way he could ride a horse now—that was an exclusive luxury reserved for the privileged upper class. The poor walked, the penitents walked, Christ walked, Francis, too, would walk.[4]

While he walked, he prayed. In a short time, the sadness of leaving his beloved city and family subsided and a feeling of freedom began to set in. He began to feel more and more confident in himself, his calling, and his new life. He decided to stop asking himself what he would do with his life—whether he would be great or not.

At times, the song of the spirit flooded his mind and he began to sing in French, the language of the troubadours. Then he would pick up two sticks and act as if he were playing a violin.[5] He started to feel like a wandering minstrel, a vagabond poet, a troubadour following his dream.

---

4 Francis would eventually write in his Rule of 1221 that friars should not travel by horse; they were to walk in the penitential tradition. See "The Earlier Rule," in *Francis and Clare: The Complete Works*, trans. Regis J. Armstrong (Mahwah, NJ: Paulist Press, 1982), chap. 15.

5 See Thomas of Celano, "The Remembrance of the Desire of a Soul," in *Francis of Assisi: Early Documents*, vol. 2, *The Founder*, chap. 90, 127.

He praised God and began to feel encouraged for the future. Now that he had completely separated himself from his former way of life, God's presence began to fill his soul as never before. The graces he had experienced before he separated from his father had been a trickle; now they amounted to a flood.

Whereas he had been half asleep before, now he felt fully awake. Things that used to bother him suddenly vanished. He felt set free.

Walking allowed Francis to observe the world around him from a different perspective. It connected him to the earth in a special way that was impossible while riding horseback or traveling by carriage. While walking, he felt connected to the land as if he were a part of the land.

He found the rhythmic tapping of his boots on the rocky dirt trails and roads to be prayerful, almost contemplative. He looked around at the rocks, trees, birds, fields, and creation. He had just given up all his possessions to follow God in freedom and poverty. And now he began to feel a kinship with the things around him.

He had now come to believe in God's omnipotent and omnipresent love, and he began to realize that everything created by God came from that same immense love—that all creation flows from God's love. For Francis, to walk around in nature was to rejoice in God as he felt God's love and grace pouring down upon him. His response was to praise God.

The land to the north of Assisi—toward Gubbio—was quite hilly and mountainous. Francis loved the mountains. They reminded him of God's power and omnipotence.

As Francis ascended the mountains, he stopped to absorb himself in prayer in the caves. He looked up at the forest, dense with holly, holm oaks, and beech trees. He felt his spirit soar higher and higher with each step up.

The mountain forests seemed to Francis sacred, mystical, hallowed, and spiritual. He looked down and admired the spectacular vistas in the valley below. He breathed in God's goodness and praised God with his entire being.

Francis walked through the terraced mountainside olive groves. The trees—symbols of peace—seemed sacred to Francis. Their ancient, twisted trunks with deep roots reminded him of the old monks in the monasteries. "They are planted in the house of the LORD, / they flourish in the courts of our God. / They still bring forth fruit in old age, / they are ever full of sap and green, / to show that the LORD is upright; / he is my rock, and there is no unrighteousness in him" (Ps 92:13–15).

He reflected on how the oil pressed from the trees' fruit nourished and blessed the people through cooking and the benedictions of the priests. The olive trees with their contorted and split trunks seemed to be in pain, and Francis recognized that all the prophets suffer. While their feet were planted in this world, their spirits contemplated the things of heaven, causing them to say things that those with roots only in this world did not wish to hear.

At times, Francis stopped to talk with the old farmers, though he could barely understand them as they spoke in heavy dialect. They exuded an earthy spirituality and genuine humility: land, earth—*humus*, humble. Francis recognized them as mystics even if they themselves probably did not.

In their work on the fields, their lives were intimately connected to light and darkness, heat and cold, and the rhythm of the seasons. In the winter, they plowed and sowed; in the spring, they cut the grass; in the summer, they harvested wheat and grains; in the fall, they picked grapes and olives. The annual cycle of growth, harvest, and reseeding was like the life, death, and resurrection of Christ in the Paschal mystery.

The farmers understood the meaning of that verse: "Truly, truly, I say to you, unless a grain of wheat falls into the earth and dies, it remains alone; but if it dies, it bears much fruit" (Jn 12:24). Francis befriended a farmer to whom he told his story. He recounted the ugliness of his sins and the fallout with his family, but now he was living a beautiful spiritual life dedicated to imitating Christ and being minor.

The farmer listened quietly and, when Francis finished, simply said, "Manure fertilizes the land and makes the crops grow." Francis understood and smiled. He used to consider peasants dull and ignorant. Instead, they were blessed with a sacred life.

Francis began observing creation and, in doing so, learning about God. For by observing creation, one can learn about the Creator. In creation, Francis saw the hand of God, the reflection of God. He began to view creation as incarnational—even sacramental. God's creation reminded him of Scripture:

> You visit the earth and water it,
> make it abundantly fertile.

God's stream is filled with water;
you supply their grain.
Thus do you prepare it:
you drench its plowed furrows,
and level its ridges.
With showers you keep it soft,
blessing its young sprouts.
You adorn the year with your bounty;
your paths drip with fruitful rain.
The meadows of the wilderness also drip,
the hills are robed with joy.
The pastures are clothed with flocks,
the valleys blanketed with grain;
they cheer and sing for joy. (Ps 65:10–14 NABRE)

Francis was too awed by the majesty of the Creator's work to ever have fallen into the dualistic beliefs of the Cathar heretics, though they were widespread in that region and in his era. The Cathars held to the idea of two gods: a good god of the spirit and a bad god of matter. They saw the good god only in the invisible spiritual world, while they believed the created material world to be the rotten fruit of the evil material god. Thus they embraced spiritual poverty and spurned material things.

Francis, on the other hand, saw all creation as good. All creation had to be good, since it was created by the one good God. The first chapter of the first book of the Bible made it clear that the world was created good: "And God saw everything that he had made, and behold, it was very good" (Gn 1:31).

The New Testament built on that, stating that the material world was good also because creation took place through the Word: "All things were made through him, and without him was not anything made that was made" (Jn 1:3); "He is the image of the invisible God, the firstborn of all creation; for in him all things were created, in heaven and on earth, visible and invisible . . . all things were created through him and for him" (Col 1:15–16). The Creed of Nicaea clarified this truth, saying, "Through [the Word] all things were made."

When Francis prayed the *Pater Noster* (Our Father), he was declaring that all people around him were fraternal, sharing the same Father. In fact, he saw Christ most of all in other human beings, since people, more than all of creation, were made in the image of God (cf. Gn 1:27). Yet as Francis considered himself and people part of creation, he began to consider even animals and inanimate objects as his brothers and sisters, too. He was especially fond of the lesser parts of nature. Whenever he found little worms on a road, he would gently pick them up and move them to safety, lest they be crushed underfoot.[6]

Francis continued walking. During the day, he learned to have a deep respect for the sun. It was particularly cold that spring, but when the sun was out and shining, it warmed Francis' body. How powerful was the sun that illumined the day and warmed his body. He came to feel a fraternal admiration for the sun. It was like a big brother who looked after him and protected him—*Frate Sole* (Brother Sun), Francis thought. He smiled.

At night, Francis would warm himself with a fire. He also felt a kinship with the warm flames, as the fire, too, was like a caring brother who covered Francis as with a blanket. There were strength and force in the flames; fire was consuming,

---

6 See Celano, "Remembrance," chap. 124, 165.

burning, powerful, handsome. *Frate Fuoco* (Brother Fire), definitely.[7]

He looked up at the moon . . . how beautiful she was, too. Yes, *Sora Luna* (Sister Moon). Together with the stars, the celestial bodies were shiny, precious, and beautiful.

Francis stopped to drink from the rivers and streams. How chaste and precious water was. He thought of Christ's baptism. The Baptizer was correct in saying, "I need to be baptized by you, and do you come to me?" (Mt 3:14). When Christ was baptized by water, nothing changed in Christ; *Christ* did not need redemption, *the world* did. And indeed, Christ's baptism did not transform *him*; instead, it redeemed the *water*. Consequently, all of creation was redeemed in Christ's baptism. *Sora Acqua* (Sister Water), Francis thought.

Yes, all things were created through Christ and redeemed by Christ. In fact, the Word—through whom all creation was made—became man. And in that becoming man, Christ redeemed the fallen nature of the world.

So wherever Francis looked, he saw the reflection of the incarnate Christ. For Francis, creation was more than good; it was sacramental. Francis praised God for the elements of his creation.

Francis lay down in a quiet, warm field next to the road and gazed at it all. He smiled at the extraordinary beauty of the rolling fields with the backdrop of the mountains. Brother Sun overhead drew out the strong fragrance of the

---

7 Here I suggest that Francis began to formulate the themes for his famous poem/prayer, *The Canticle of the Creatures*. In reality, we know that he wrote it toward the end of his life when he was near death and staying in a hut near San Damiano.

pine, fig, and juniper trees. The wafts of wild lavender, rosemary, mint, and other herbs created an aroma more pleasant than the finest perfume he had ever smelled at the fairs of France. The playful butterflies, darting lizards, and twittering larks seemed just as happy as he was.

The earth was now his mother, *Matre Terra*. How beautiful she was with her colored flowers, fruits, and herbs. She would now sustain him with her grain, wheat, and herbs. Francis had given up a little, but had truly received a hundredfold already in this life (cf. Mk 10:29–30). "Laudato sie, mi Signore cum tucte le Tue creature" (Praised be you, my Lord, for all your creatures), he thought to himself.

How he praised God for all his creatures! Yes, Francis was a nature mystic and he would preach to the birds from time to time. Yet underlying his relationship to the world was a thoroughly and profoundly Christian theology rooted in the Father as Creator and the Son as Redeemer. He never praised the works of creation in and of themselves; instead, he praised God *per* his creation.

Francis' thoughts were suddenly interrupted by the noisy sound of galloping horses. He turned to see some well-dressed young men ride by, scattering the animals. They were shouting foul language and were so excited and angered by something that they never even noticed Francis laying there.

Francis' thoughts quickly shifted toward his family and the people of Assisi. He felt a twinge of sadness and he missed them. But he knew he was on the right path. He had no regrets. He got up and continued walking.

At times, Francis felt tired. His legs and feet frequently hurt. Sometimes he was even bored. But he recognized that difficulties would be part of the journey. The spiritual life would not be lived exclusively up on the mountaintop; most of it would be lived down in the plains of the daily toil of life.

Other times, he felt apprehensive for the future, and he would get anxious. How would he be provided for? Where would his food and shelter come from?

But by now, he was learning to turn to God for everything. When he did turn to God, the appropriate thought would come to his mind. He would be reminded of Scripture: "And why are you anxious about clothing? Consider the lilies of the field, how they grow; they neither toil nor spin; yet I tell you, even Solomon in all his glory was not arrayed like one of these. But if God so clothes the grass of the field, which today is alive and tomorrow is thrown into the oven, will he not much more clothe you, O men of little faith?" (Mt 6:28–30).

Yes, he had faith that he would be taken care of.

While journeying with his father and entourage in the past, they usually slept at the inns. However, from time to time, when inns were not available, they would be forced to accept accommodations in the Benedictine monasteries. The monks were always hospitable, as hospitality was part of the Rule of St. Benedict. They would take in anyone— pilgrims, merchants, knights, wanderers, and penitents.

Francis knew of such a monastery in San Verecondo, a few miles south of Gubbio. He went there and stayed for some time. The monks provided him with food and lodging in exchange for help in the kitchen.[8]

---

8 The only thirteenth-century source to mention Francis' short sojourn with the monks is Thomas of Celano, "The Life of Saint Francis," in

In the monastery, Francis enjoyed being surrounded by a community of believers. They gave him a sense of peace and consolation. With their long beards, flowing black tunics, scapulars, cowls, and leather belts and boots, the monks deeply impressed him. He appreciated their liturgical celebrations, rich with incense, bells, and chant. He learned much about Christian life and community from the great Rule of St. Benedict, and Francis' devotion to Scripture deepened in the constant chanting of the Psalms. Francis hoped that one day he would have a community like that of San Verecondo.

But Francis understood very quickly that his vocation was not to the monastic life. Monasticism based on *stabilitas* (stability) rooted it to a fixed portion of land. The monastic enclosure was too restrictive and established for Francis, who still had too much wanderlust, even if of a spiritual sort now.

Over time, many abbeys had become powerful, their expansive estates quite endowed. Feudalism was still very much alive in many of them. Francis had just rejected the patrimony of his father, and he was not going to swap one form of security for another.

Francis of Assisi: Early Documents, ed. and trans. Regis J. Armstrong, vol. 1, *The Saint* (Hyde Park, NY: New City Press, 1999), chap. 7, 16. Thomas mentions a "certain cloister of monks" that he describes as an unhappy experience for Francis, who was forced to work as a kitchen-hand for several morsels of bread. The monastery was not mentioned by name by Thomas; however, it was most likely San Verecondo. Today it has been refurbished into an agritourism vacation area with a plaque mentioning Francis' stay. Despite Francis' ill treatment, I have offered a more positive perspective.

The silent monastery with its icons, religious artwork, furnishings, and decorations was suitable for prayer, he thought. But God's creation was the perfect place for him to be alone and meditate. Nature with her panoramas of the sky, mountains, and valleys would be his cloister, not the manmade walls of the monastery.

Yes, Francis' spirituality would be lived itinerantly in poverty on the open road, where he would announce the gospel to anyone who would listen. He would live just like Jesus' first apostles. Even though he had disassociated himself from his father's business and ways, he was still a merchant at heart.

Francis had just sold everything he had to buy the most precious Pearl that neither rust nor moth could destroy (cf. Mt 6:20). He was not about to bury it in a field within a monastic enclosure. No, he would travel far and wide to freely give it away to anyone who desired it.

He would live with no fixed abode. He would be a jongleur, a vagabond poet, a troubadour, a wandering minstrel roaming about in song, striving only to help the poor and needy and preach the gospel. Francis left the monastery and continued his journey with praise and joy in his heart.

Francis finally arrived in Gubbio, a wealthy mercantile city then flourishing in the cloth trade. Gubbio was guarded by its great patron saint, Ubaldo, whose relics remain enshrined in the church atop Mount Ingino overlooking the city. Francis knew Gubbio well. He had a merchant friend who lived there named Federico Spadalunga.

They had fought together in the battle against Perugia. His name, meaning "long sword," was a testament to his time spent in battle. Federico offered Francis hospitality and gave him a new tunic.[9]

In Gubbio, Francis served lepers and prayed in the hermitages in the hills. After a few months, however, he realized he could not continue as a wanderer. The roads, city squares, and inns were full of those types. Many started out as honest Christians with a sincere intention to spread the gospel but ended up as errant ne'er-do-wells.

His beloved Assisi had never left Francis' heart. He missed the olive groves of San Damiano, the larks of the valley, the caves of the Carceri, the townspeople, and, above all, his lepers of Arce. But more than anything else, there was that voice he could not get out of his mind. He decided to go back to Assisi with something constructive in mind: *rebuild God's house.*

---

9 There are documents that state that the Spadalunga family took Francis in after he left his family and gave him shelter and a new tunic. They later built a church for the friars after the movement had grown. Part of the original Spadalunga family house is preserved within the same church, which still exists today and is now run by the Conventual Franciscans.

9

POVERTY AND
THE PORTIUNCULA

He charged them to take nothing for their journey except a
staff; no bread, no bag, no money in their belts; but to wear
sandals and not put on two tunics.

MARK 6:8–9

IT was the summer of 1206. Francis returned to Assisi
to rebuild the Church of San Damiano. Since he heard
the voice there, Francis carried a deep devotion in his
heart to churches. In fact, whenever he entered one, he
would say, "We adore You, Lord Jesus Christ, in all
Your churches throughout the world, and we bless You,
for through Your holy cross You have redeemed the
world."[1] He frequently carried a broom with him that
he used to clean churches.[2]

---

1 This is a traditional prayer inspired from the Holy Thursday liturgy.
Francis recited it upon entering churches. See St. Francis, "The Testament,"
in *Francis and Clare: The Complete Works*, trans. Regis J. Armstrong
(Mahwah, NJ: Paulist Press, 1982), 4–5.

2 Francis brought brooms with him to clean churches in the vicinity of
Assisi when he went preaching. See "The Assisi Compilation," in *Francis of Assisi: Early Documents*, ed. and trans. Regis J. Armstrong, vol. 2,
The Founder (Hyde Park, NY: New City Press, 2000), 60.

Francis had found Jesus within the particular Church of San Damiano, but in that specific church, he developed in his heart a deep love for the universal Church that he would keep throughout his entire life. For it was through the Church that he received Jesus in the Eucharist. He would eventually write in his *Testament*, "I see nothing corporally of the Most High Son of God in this world except his Most holy Body and Blood which priests receive and which priests alone administer to others."[3]

When he heard heretics blast priests and bishops for corruption or laxity, Francis never argued with them. Instead, he would simply say, "Through their blessed hands I receive Jesus."[4]

Francis went through the streets of Assisi begging for materials for the restoration of San Damiano. He also begged for oil so the lamp next to the crucifix would always be illuminated. He still had to contend with the insults of the townspeople and his brother, Angelo, from time to time. However, it was the curses of his father that pained him the most.

His father could not stand seeing his firstborn son, the one he loved the most, lowered to the condition of a city beggar. So whenever he saw Francis, his father shouted curses

---

3 Francis, "The Testament," in *Francis and Clare: The Complete Works*, 10.

4 In Francis' writings, he makes numerous references to his devotion to the Eucharist that he receives through the hands of priests. A story written by a Dominican priest in 1261 narrates how a heretic challenged Francis by asking him whether the faithful should respect the sacraments administered by a sinful priest. Francis responded by going to the priest, kissing his hands, and claiming that his hands were still a channel of God's graces.

at him. After several nasty encounters, Francis asked a poor beggar named Alberto to counteract his father's curses with blessings from God. Then he turned to his father and said, "Don't you see that my Father has given me someone whose blessings will counter your curses?"[5]

However, soon some of the townspeople began to change their mind about Francis. Perhaps it was the serenity and calm with which Francis responded to their insults. Some began to consider that perhaps Francis was not so crazy after all. They began to give him rocks, stones, and mortar to help him rebuild the church.

Having restored San Damiano, Francis set to work on another church, San Pietro in Spina, in the area of San Petrignano in the valley near Rivotorto. Francis' father owned land there and Francis knew the area.[6] Finally, he moved on to a third church, Santa Maria degli Angeli (St. Mary of the Angels). It was called the Portiuncula (little portion), as it stood on a small portion of land.[7]

---

5 See Thomas of Celano, "The Remembrance of the Desire of a Soul," in *Francis of Assisi: Early Documents*, vol. 2, *The Founder*, chap. 7, 12; the beggar's name is mentioned in Francis, "The Beginning or the Founding of the Order and the Deeds of Those Lesser Brothers Who Were the First Companions of the Blessed Francis in Religion," in *Francis of Assisi: Early Documents*, vol. 2, *The Founder*, chap. 9.

6 Bonaventure mentions the church, San Pietro in Spina (St. Peter in Spina), by name in "Major Legend." Unfortunately, the church has once again collapsed in ruin, and there is no trace of a church—just piles of stones. The ruins are on the private property of a local family who use the surrounding land as a horse farm. Bonaventure of Bagnoregio, "The Major Legend of Saint Francis," in *Francis of Assisi: Early Documents*, vol. 2, *The Founder*, chap. 2.

7 The Portiuncula (*Porziuncola* in Italian) remained the home base for Francis and the brothers after they left Rivotorto. The original little church currently stands under a large basilica in the center of St. Mary

Located in the bug-infested, swampy forest in the valley near the leper hospitals, this minor little church was broken down more than the rest. It was the perfect place for Francis. Francis loved the Portiuncula more than any other church because it was dedicated to Mary.

Francis was filled with an inexpressible love toward the Mother of Jesus because it was she who made the Lord of Majesty his brother.[8] Francis' rupture with his earthly family took place next to another church dedicated to Mary, St. Mary Major, the greatest of all the saints. Just as Mary had enveloped Jesus within her womb as a type of tabernacle, the bishop enveloped Francis in his cloak, symbolizing his complete immersion within the Church. Francis would write that it was right to honor the blessed Virgin, since she carried Jesus in her most holy womb.[9]

---

of the Angels (the town is named after the church) about two miles south of Assisi. The first basilica was built between 1569 and 1679 but was severely damaged by a nineteenth-century earthquake. The current basilica was rebuilt, and in 1909 it was declared motherhouse of the Order of Friars Minor (O.F.M.). All the ornamentation on and in the Portiuncula was added after Francis' death. Behind the Portiuncula is a little chapel that marks the place where St. Francis died. To the right is a corridor winding through a rose garden where (according to tradition) Francis once rolled around in the nude to overcome a temptation, causing the roses to later grow without thorns. Beyond the garden is a chapel where Francis slept in his hut. In July 1216, Francis had a dream in which Jesus and Mary promised him that anyone who came to the Portiuncula would receive complete remission of sins, a plenary indulgence known as the Pardon of Assisi. Traditionally the date when one could receive the indulgence was August 2, although it has now been extended to a visit on any day of the year.

8 See Celano, "Remembrance," chap. 150.

9 See St. Francis, "A Letter to the Entire Order," in *Francis and Clare: The Complete Works*, 21.

On February 24, 1208—the feast of St. Mathias—one of the most significant events in the life of the son of the wealthy merchant took place. During Mass at the Church of St. Mary of the Angels, Francis heard a Gospel reading: "Take no gold, nor silver, nor copper in your belts, no bag for your journey, nor two tunics, nor sandals, nor a staff" (Mt 10:9–10).[10] Francis sat mesmerized as the words struck him to the core.

His heart was set ablaze as his life's mission—his Rule of Life—was being revealed to him in that Scripture passage. This would be a major turning point in his life. He realized what he would do. He would embrace total poverty. He spoke to the priest after Mass, asking him to explain the Gospel reading in order to confirm what he believed was the meaning.

The priest explained that these were the words that Jesus spoke to his disciples as he commissioned them to go out and preach the gospel to all who would listen. The priest also cited Luke's Gospel: "Whoever of you does not renounce all that he has cannot be my disciple" (Lk 14:33). He explained to Francis that Jesus did not want his disciples to take anything when they went out to announce the gospel, otherwise they would not be bringing Jesus.

Worldly things would be a burden to them and would interfere with the purity of the gospel message. Jesus wanted his followers to imitate him by emptying themselves of all they possessed. They were to be without calculations, without time, without particular roles assigned.

---

10 Each of the early sources describes this event in Francis' life.

The only things they were to possess were Christ and his virtues of humility, simplicity, vulnerability, nonpossession, and generosity. They were to go simply through the villages and cities preaching the Word and being an example of the kingdom of God. This is what Francis desired and he was overjoyed.

The thought of total poverty thrilled him and filled his heart. Francis did not react to Scripture solely with his head but with his entire being and feelings. He responded to Scripture with his heart, desire, and immediacy, taking the Word literally and allowing it to move him and his life.

Yes, poverty is what he wanted and desired with all his existence. Total poverty. These few Gospel words would define Francis' mission for the rest of his life and would also become the vocation of his followers. Francis would live in total poverty as Jesus himself demanded of his apostles in Scripture.

Poverty made sense to Francis as the best way to live the Christian life and to be an example. In his worldly life as a merchant, he had observed so many people inordinately attached to material things. Many were greedy and avaricious. Yet even within the Church, the canons and monks from privileged backgrounds were also sometimes puffed up with their status, culture, education, and property.

This did not resonate well among the simple faithful. The clerics' battles in the tribunals in defense of their property and privileges were not good evangelization. Francis would seek to be different—he would possess nothing other than Jesus.

Francis' desire to embrace poverty originated in his desire to imitate the self-emptying nature of God himself: the

Christ who descended from heaven, emptying himself; the Christ who was born a defenseless child in a stable; the Christ who was raised by lowly parents; the Christ who worked with his hands; the Christ who died on the cross; the Christ who became the Eucharist; the Christ who saves.

Poverty for Francis was emptying himself of the things of the world in order to embrace God fully. Poverty was not a value in and of itself but was self-emptying to become full of God and God's love. Being poor would allow him to be full of God's graces wherever and whenever they were given to him.

Francis' life of poverty would not be a flight from the world, a *fuga mundi*. He did not hate the world or believe it to be evil, as did the Cathars. Francis believed creation—the cosmos—was good, as it was created so by the Creator. The world was as a reflection, a sign, even a sacrament of what was beyond.

With that mind-set, Francis often perceived spiritual things that most people could not, since he saw God's reflection in creation. It was easy for Francis to praise God and sing of his goodness in the world when he was not attached to the world. The worldliness he rejected was not the world in and of itself but rather the mentality of the world—the mind-set of the current age.

The Lord had warned his disciples to not belong to the world any more than he belonged to the world (see Jn 17:16). Francis would love the world and see in creation the work of the Creator. Yet within the world, he would reject the work of the Evil One.

Francis would make poverty his Rule of Life. In the first sentence of his Rule of Life, he would one day write, "The

Rule and Life of the Lesser Brothers is this: to observe the Holy Gospel of Our Lord Jesus Christ by living in obedience, without anything of one's own [*sine proprio*], and in chastity."[11] The words *sine proprio* made up a common technical and legal term describing the vow of poverty as one of the three evangelical counsels common already in other Rules in the twelfth century. Yet they had deeper meaning for Francis.

For Francis, poverty was more than simply not possessing material things. Poverty for Francis would require detachment from everything—material or spiritual—that interfered with God's ability to reach him. It included the senses, possessiveness, even relationships.

Since he would not seek to cling to or selfishly possess anything, he naturally felt a fraternal relationship to everything and everyone. He moved away from the social system in which people related to one another in the traditional lord-subject manner. No, Francis would be on equal par with others as his brothers and sisters.

Poverty was about attitudes, inner dispositions, and values as much as it was about material wealth or the lack of it. It referred not merely to a way of life devoid of material possessions but to a soul that was free of self, liberated from selfish desires, willing to let go of ambition, and surrendered to God's will. "Without anything of one's own" meant remaining serene and peaceful and detached from the state of being of others despite their sins, defects, or vices. He would write, "That servant of God who does not

---

11 St. Francis, "The Later Rule," in *Francis and Clare: The Complete Works*, 136.

become angry or upset at anything, lives justly and without anything of his own [*sine proprio*]."[12]

Poverty would include a willingness to detach from nonmaterial things around him—even when those things were good. Francis would write, "No minister or preacher may appropriate to himself a ministry of the brothers or the office of preaching; they should humbly surrender them when required to do so."[13] Thus even when serving God and doing God's will, Francis felt he could sin against poverty if he was too attached to such service.

Ultimately, Francis believed that nothing was his own. Everything he came into contact with originated in God and would one day return to God. The opposite of poverty was clinging or grasping to one's will, storing up treasures and possessing.

Francis never believed money or wealth to be the root of all sin. He believed that the worst sin was in "appropriating to one's self" what was not one's to have: "For that person eats of the tree of the knowledge of good who appropriates his will to himself and, in this way, exalts himself over the good things the Lord says and does in him."[14] In other words, true poverty for Francis was in only accepting the will of God and nothing more.

Filled with joy at his new calling, he wasted no time in carrying out literally what he heard in that Scripture reading.

---

12 St. Francis, "The Admonitions," in *Francis and Clare: The Complete Works*, chap. 11.

13 St. Francis, "Fragments Found in a Manuscript in the Worchester Cathedral," in *Francis of Assisi: Early Documents*, ed. and trans. Regis J. Armstrong, vol. 1, *The Saint* (Hyde Park, NY: New City Press, 1999), 87.

14 Francis, "Admonitions," chap. 2.

He promptly put down his heavy stick. He removed his heavy wooden shoes and put on crude sandals. He replaced his penitent's tunic with a shepherd's cloak. He substituted the heavy leather hermit's belt with a cord, to which no possessions could be attached.

He was now transformed from a hermit-penitent into an apostolic preacher. He became the *poverello*, "the poor little one," who would joyfully proclaim the kingdom of God in total poverty.

10

EVANGELIZATION AND BROTHER BERNARD

If you would be perfect, go, sell what you possess and give to the poor, and you will have treasure in heaven; and come, follow me.

MATTHEW 19:21

B ERNARD, the son of Quintavalle di Berardello, was a highly respected merchant from a noble family. He was known for his nobility and wealth, but above all for his culture and learning. He held degrees in both civil and canon law, and he was well respected for his counsel.

His home was not far from the house Francis grew up in. It was just below the Piazza del Commune, next to the Church of San Gregorio.[1] Bernard had known Francis

---

1 The actual house of Bernard of Quintavalle still stands today. Francis and Bernard lived together in the first days at Rivotorto and the Portiuncula; they traveled to Rome, France, and Spain together; and he was present in the moments of Francis' death. St. Bonaventure later described him as the "firstborn son" of the saint. The house was originally built by Bernardo's family in the twelfth century over some old Roman ruins. It was one of a series of tall, narrow, tower-like fortresses, called *casini*, commonly built in clusters. In the sixteenth century, an Assisian noble family, Sbaraglini, bought the land and tore down the surrounding tower houses, leaving the Bernardo house for its spiritual importance. The family then built the

when the now-penitent was still working with his father. He was also present at the bishop's residence to watch the two separate forever. He watched Francis in his transformation from a carefree youth destined to become a knight and conquer the world into the poor beggar he had become.

Many of the townspeople of Assisi were still bent on deriding Francis. When his name came up in conversation, they would say *pazzo* (crazy) and tap the side of their head with their index finger. "Only crazy people voluntarily give up wealth to become beggars. Most people become poor through misfortune like disease, or the death of their fathers or husbands, or they lose their house or shop in a fire." They felt sorry for Pietro, but more so for Francis' mother, Pica.

Bernard, too, was confused when he watched Francis. He did not believe Francis was insane; there were plenty of truly crazy people wandering around the streets of Assisi, but Francis was not one of them. Crazy people had hollow eyes that just stared off. Francis' eyes exuded a confidence and joy that were difficult to comprehend.

Yet Bernard's legal mind—trained to distinguish between reason and irrationality, good and evil, wisdom and foolishness—had not yet fully understood the transformation of Francis. It was not reasonable for a person

---

adjacent Renaissance-style mansion and adjoined it to the Bernardo house. The house is composed of three floors, each about thirty by thirty feet. The upper room, where the story from "The Little Flowers of Saint Francis" took place, has been converted into a chapel. In 2001, the last descendant carrying the Sbaraglini name died, and the house was for sale for many years.

to withstand the jeers of their fellow townspeople with the peace Francis bore it.

Bernard had rarely witnessed people like Francis who put their faith into practice. Sure, the churches were packed on Sundays and feast days, but hardly anyone received the Eucharist or ever went to confession.[2] Most people seemed more concerned with what others were wearing and doing, while paying little attention to the Mass. Or they flocked to relic processions and rituals in honor of the saints in hope of receiving a blessing. Most seemed more interested in what they could get out of this life and did not seem concerned about what they could give. Though they claimed to follow Christ, so many believers seemed to be running after something else.

But the bitter truth for Bernard was that when he looked in the mirror, he saw himself as one of them. He, too, had been catechized in the faith but had never been happy with his life. Like Francis, he had been trained in the ways of business and commerce. And when Bernard was honest with himself, he realized that he, too, had engaged in certain behaviors that went against his beliefs.

Money and power had taken hold of him, and his conscience told him that the things he had done in order to acquire more of it or to keep what he had were wrong. His heart was not at peace. Francis, on the other hand, Bernard observed, seemed to have an inner serenity.

One day, Bernard saw Francis begging for supplies in the streets of Assisi. He had finished rebuilding two churches

---

2 The so-called Easter duty was instituted in 1215 in the Fourth Lateran Council by Pope Innocent III, requiring the faithful to receive communion and confess one's sins at least at Easter.

and was now working on a third down in the valley—
St. Mary of the Angels. Francis announced to anyone who
would listen, "The stone the builders rejected has become
the cornerstone!" (cf. Ps 118:22). "Does anyone wish to
give your worthless materials to God? Stone, mortar,
gravel? How about you, Bernard of Quintavalle? Do you
care to help rebuild God's house?"

Bernard responded that he did. He invited Francis to his
house that evening for supper.[3] Francis, for his part, discerned in Bernard's manner that he had something other
than rocks on his mind. He accepted the invitation.

The two sat down to dinner in Bernard's luxurious palace, replete with servants. A warm fire was lit in the hearth.
Francis was seated in the place of honor—just as in the past
when he had been head of the merrymakers.

The two were served locally hunted meat and game with
sauces and spices. Francis ate what was given to him in
deference to his host, though he had long ago renounced
such feasts. Now he was accustomed to eating what the
peasants ate—soup with bread and vegetables and occasionally pork.

Over dinner, Bernard recounted to Francis how he felt
about his life, how he felt enslaved to money, status, power,
and the expectations of others. He said he was a Christian,
but he had never felt free to deeply follow Christ. Francis
listened without interjecting much. He did not have to say

---

3 See "The Little Flowers of Saint Francis," in *Francis of Assisi: Early
Documents*, ed. and trans. Regis J. Armstrong, vol. 3, *The Prophet* (Hyde
Park, NY: New City Press, 2001), chap. 2, for the story of Bernard's
conversion.

anything, as his life now witnessed to Bernard that there was another way to live the Christian life.

Francis then spoke by saying how his life had been fulfilled just as he had hoped. He had become a knight and he was married to a lady and was serving a Lord. But he was a knight of Christ serving God and the lady he married was Lady Poverty.

After dinner, they prayed together and then retired to bed. Francis noticed that Bernard seemed hopeful.

Bernard offered Francis a spare bed in his room, where an oil lamp burned throughout the night. The luxurious bed had two sheets and a mattress stuffed with straw and covered with furs; the comfortable pillow was stuffed with feathers. A set of freshly cleaned, ironed, and folded undergarments were on the bed for Francis.

In deference to his host, Francis lay down on the comfortable bed, though he had taken up the custom of sleeping in boxes filled with hay—like the poor—and using rocks for pillows. Francis waited for Bernard to fall asleep so he could get up and pray privately. When Francis heard him snoring, he arose from his bed, went to the window, and there he prayed. He repeated over and over throughout the night the same words, "My God and my all."

Meanwhile, Bernard had only pretended to be asleep and was really watching Francis.

Bernard was amazed at the sanctity of his guest. Here was a true follower of Christ. Francis possessed something different.

Bernard rolled over and stared up into the darkness, ruminating about his life. How had he done the things he had done? How had he lived that way as long as he had?

As he lay there that night, he felt a new desire within him begin to burn. It was something different and fresh, something he had not felt in a long time. He began to feel the passion burning within his heart to do what Francis was doing.

Bernard yearned to live like him. He, too, now felt the gospel call to give up everything he had in order to follow Christ, like Francis. He wanted that same peace and joy. Bernard was finished living his life the way he wanted. Yes, he would live as God wanted. Like Francis.

When the sun came up in the morning and the bells of San Gregorio began to ring, Bernard told Francis of his intentions. Francis was amazed and humbled at the same time. To discern God's will, together they went up the street to the little Church of San Nicola on the western side of the marketplace square, and there they consulted the Gospels.

They asked the priest to open the altar missal three times at random.[4] They read the following Scriptures: "Si vis perfectus esse vade vende quae habes et da pauperibus et habebis thesaurum in caelo et veni sequere me" (Mt 19:21; If you would be perfect, go, sell what you possess and give to the poor, and you will have treasure in heaven; and come, follow me), "Nihil tuleritis in via" (Lk 9:3; Take nothing for your journey), and "Si quis vult post me venire abneget se ipsum et tollat crucem suam cotidie et sequatur me" (Lk 9:23; If any man would come after

---

4 This practice of opening of the Bible at random to discern God's will was known as a *sortes biblicae*. It was considered superstitious by church leaders and theologians who debated whether it should even be done; yet it was quite frequently practiced by the laity.

me, let him deny himself and take up his cross daily and follow me).

The two young Assisians looked at each other and Francis said to Bernard, "Brother, this is our life and our rule. You know what to do." Without hesitation, Bernard did exactly what the Scriptures told him to do.[5]

Bernard went immediately back to his house and brought out all his possessions—and he was very rich. He did exactly what the Gospel told him to do and sold all that he owned. With great enthusiasm and joy, Francis and Bernard gave all his money to the people of Assisi. Life would no longer be comfortable, influential, or successful for the first follower of Francis. Yet Bernard was filled with joy at such a prospect.

The remarkable thing about Bernard's conversion is that Francis had never actively sought to proselytize or convince others to join him. His only wish was to do the will of the Lord and to follow Christ as he felt led. Yet Francis was not opposed to living in community with others who wanted to live like him. And when Bernard desired to follow him, he accepted.

Francis' evangelization was primarily through his example. He believed that evangelization took place not only in the words he said but more so through the fullness of the gospel in the way he lived his life. More convincing than persuasive arguments—perhaps the most powerful instrument he had in evangelization—was his transformed life.

---

5 The actual missal that Bernard and Francis opened is today, curiously, conserved within the Walters Art Museum of Baltimore, Maryland.

For Francis, being an evangelist is not something he *did* or *said*; it is what he *became*. Francis always sought to live the gospel first and preach second.[6] He believed that preaching should be done by his deeds.[7] He believed that words should be well chosen, pure, and brief, because it was in few words that the Lord preached while on earth.[8]

Certainly, Francis believed that it was important and necessary to speak the gospel. Yet he believed preaching and evangelization should first reflect what was in his heart. When his heart was on fire for the Lord, his words would be

---

6 There is a popular statement attributed to St. Francis: "Preach the Gospel at all times and when necessary use words." It comes from a story that goes like this: St. Francis once said to a novice, "Brother, let us go into Assisi and preach." Together they went up into the city and quietly walked through the streets. But Francis never said a word to any of the bystanders on the streets, even though many looked on curiously at the strangely clad men. After they exited through the city gate and headed back down to the friary of St. Mary of the Angels, the novice was confused. "And what about preaching, brother Francis?" he asked. "It is done," replied the saint, "when we witness to others the joy and beauty of our evangelical life in our simplicity, in addition to the care and concern we have shown for one another. Thus, our example is often the most eloquent kind of preaching. Remember this, young friar: Preach the Gospel at all times and when necessary use words." This last sentence is one of the most quoted phrases by St. Francis; it is found all over the internet, on T-shirts, even on bumper stickers. However, St. Francis never actually said it; the story does not appear in any of the original thirteenth-century sources. Yet its spirit is consistent with Francis' style of evangelization.

7 Francis wrote, "All the brothers, however, should preach by their deeds." "The Earlier Rule," in *Francis and Clare: The Complete Works*, trans. Regis J. Armstrong (Mahwah, NJ: Paulist Press, 1982), chap. 17, 3.

8 See Francis, "The Later Rule," in *Francis and Clare: The Complete Works*, chap. 9, 3.

on fire for the Lord. Francis would later say, "The preacher must first draw from secret prayers what he will later pour out in holy sermons; he must first grow hot within before he speaks words that are in themselves cold."[9]

For Francis, the only requirement for evangelization was to have had an experience of God—an encounter with God. Francis never believed that specialized or formal training was required to preach—evangelists were not doctors or lawyers. No, he evangelized by simply living the fullness of his Christian life.

Before announcing Christ, one had to imitate Christ; before proclaiming the gospel, one had to live the gospel; before exhorting others to do penance, one should be a penitent. Then one could be an evangelizer. All one had to do was walk the path of penance and poverty, embrace the cross, serve the marginalized, pray, and receive the sacraments.

Francis was indeed an evangelist. When people saw Francis, they saw joy, peace, serenity, goodness, and love. In effect, they saw God within him. Goodness spread. This is what the people wanted. And this is what Bernard desired.

Bernard of Quintavalle gave Francis hope. His desire to follow Francis confirmed that he was following the will of God. Francis always spoke highly of Bernard of Quinta-valle. Before he died, he said to Brother Leo:

> Write this just as I tell you: Brother Bernard was the first brother whom the Lord gave me, as well as the first to put into practice and fulfill most completely the perfection of the Holy

---

9 Thomas of Celano, "The Remembrance of the Desire of a Soul," in *Francis of Assisi: Early Documents*, ed. and trans. Regis J. Armstrong, vol. 2, *The Founder* (Hyde Park, NY: New City Press, 2000), chap. 122, 163.

Gospel by distributing all his goods to the poor; because of this and many other prerogatives, I am bound to love him more than any other brother of the entire order. Therefore, as much as I can, I desire and command that, whoever the minister general is, he should cherish and honor him as he would me, and likewise the ministers provincial and the brothers of the entire order should esteem him in place of me.[10]

---

10 St. Francis, "A Mirror of the Perfection, *Rule*, Profession, Life, and True Calling of a Lesser Brother," in *Francis of Assisi: Early Documents*, vol. 3, *The Prophet*, chap. 9, 207.

11

COMMUNITY AND RIVOTORTO

Now the company of those who believed were of one heart
and soul, and no one said that any of the things which he
possessed was his own, but they had everything in common.

ACTS 4:32

T HE three biblical verses read in the Church of San
Nicholas would become the basis of the evangelical
life the brothers were to embrace together. A fourth could
have been added: "It is not good that the man should be
alone" (Gn 2:18). And God provided.

In the summer of 1209, Peter Catani joined Francis with
Bernard. Like Bernard, he too was trained in law.[1] Then
came Giles, a poor peasant from the valley.

The friars would live poorly and itinerantly. They would
preach, serve others, and beg alms when necessary. Their

---

1 In "The Legend of the Three Companions," in *Francis of Assisi: Early
Documents*, ed. and trans. Regis J. Armstrong, vol. 2, *The Founder* (Hyde
Park, NY: New City Press, 2000), chap. 28, Peter appears together with
Bernard and all three read the scriptures together. In "The Little Flowers of
Saint Francis," in *Francis of Assisi: Early Documents*, ed. and trans. Regis
J. Armstrong, vol. 3, *The Prophet* (Hyde Park, NY: New City Press, 2001),
chap. 2, Francis is alone with Bernard.

lives were modeled after Jesus and the disciples they read about in Scripture, the *Vita Apostolica.*

They soon set out "two by two" and left Assisi on their first mission (cf. Mk 6:7). Francis and Giles went to the Marches of Ancona, while Peter and Bernard went in another direction.[2] Out of Assisi through the Parlascio gate toward the mountain pass set out two strangely dressed, sandal-clad young men. They followed the Tescio River to Piano della Pieve and went through the cities of Gualdo and then Fossato.

As they hiked through the valleys in the shadows of the rugged Apennine Mountain peaks, they breathed in the fresh mountain air. It was the beginning of the summer, and they marveled at the fields already rich in grains and cereals. They ate wild herbs, lentils, and raw fava beans and drank from streams. The Holy Spirit had set their hearts aflame with the love of God, and they praised God's goodness everywhere.

They sang and preached to the people of the hill towns and mountain villages. Giles spoke in his native Assisian dialect, while Francis sang in Provençal French, the language of the country he was named after, the language of inspiration and love, the language of his mother, and the *lingua franca*—the common language in that era.

Finally, they reached the mountain city of Fabriano. Francis knew some noblemen there with whom he had fought in the battle against Perugia. The two stayed with them for some time before returning to Assisi.[3]

---

2 See "Three Companions," chap. 9, 33.

3 The region of the Marches of Ancona is known as the Land of the Fioretti, as "The Little Flowers of Saint Francis" was written there. The region has a long Franciscan history beginning with Francis' first missionary

The local people had never witnessed such a thing. They were accustomed to either the profane or the sacred: the traveling minstrels passed through the cities performing with their delightful worldly *chanson* love songs in French, or else the preachers professed weighty Latinate sermons that the people could not understand. But here was both one and the other.

Francis was a religious preacher who sang like a minstrel. But he did not sing of a dame, king, or nobleman of this world; he exalted Lady Poverty, the King of kings, and the highest of all Lords. And he did it in a way they could understand.

Francis spoke to their hearts and their humanity, arousing their souls as he told them to love and fear God and to do penance for their sins. He did not speak down to them but addressed the people as his brothers and sisters. Most people had a difficult time seeing themselves (and others) as good, but Francis helped them look inside and see that precious pearl within.

In the end, it was not Francis himself who spoke to them. It was the Holy Spirit. Many of them awoke from a deep slumber.

When the brothers returned to Assisi, they took up residence together in some farmer's sheds in the valley below Assisi in an area known as Rivotorto. Its name

---

journey in 1208, narrated here when he had only three followers. Francis visited the region six times in his life on preaching tours and journeys to and from the Holy Land and the city of Ancona. Here the Order flourished and its contemplative side took root. Paul Sabatier, a pioneer of Franciscan studies, said, "The Marches of Ancona became and remained the province more truly Franciscan than every other."

meant "crooked stream," as a creek flowed nearby.[4] Soon after they returned to Rivotorto, the first priest arrived—Sylvester, a canon priest from the Cathedral of San Rufino. Then came more—Sabbatino, Morico, Giovanni, Filippo, and others still.

Rivotorto was the perfect place for the minor brothers. In the warm months, it was bug-infested and sweltering; in the cold months, wet and bone-chilling. Their living quarters were made up of two enclosed huts conjoined by a covered space in the middle.

They slept in one of the huts, which was so small they had to draw chalk marks on the ceiling to designate the place where each would sleep. They prayed spontaneously and charismatically in the center space, as they had not yet adopted the formal prayer of the Liturgy of the Hours. In the other hut, they cooked the wild turnips that they grew or that were given to them by the local peasants, who were just as poor.[5] The men spent time serving the lepers in the nearby hospitals of Arce.

In Rivotorto, Francis and the brothers began to experience their Christian vocation, not in solitude but in community. Francis would spend the rest of his life in community with others—often in very close quarters—and would

---

4 Today Rivotorto is the name of a large basilica as well as the small town located about two miles from St. Mary of the Angels. Inside the basilica (completely rebuilt in neo-Gothic style after an earthquake in 1854) are several huts reconstructed to look like the original dwellings where Francis and the first friars lived. Although the original location is unknown, it was in the general location of the present church. The church is overseen today by the Conventual Franciscans.

5 See "Three Companions," chap. 13, 55.

hardly do anything alone. In community, the brothers would live a way of life directly following the Holy Gospel, as their way of life was modeled after that of Jesus and the first disciples.[6] They could not live the gospel in isolation; it had to be lived out in the context of others.

For Francis, his companions were a gift from the Lord. In fraternity, each brother brought with him the gift of himself. In fact, the fraternity would not have been the same without each particular brother. Each man would enrich the group in a particular way with the particular gifts God had given him.

Francis often spoke of his brothers and their gifts.[7] He spoke of the simplicity and purity of Leo (Francis' secretary and confessor); the courtesy of Angelo; the gracious disposition, eloquence, and natural sense of Masseo; the contemplative spirit of Giles; the virtuous and constant prayer of Rufino; the patience of Juniper.[8] Brother James had a devotion to the lepers that was perhaps greater than even Francis', Brother Simone had the gift of deep spiritual contemplation, Brother Tebaldo was known for miracles, Brother Agostino had a reputation for saintliness, Brother Pacifico was called the "King of Verses."

---

6 See St. Francis, "The Testament," in *Francis and Clare: The Complete Works*, trans. Regis J. Armstrong (Mahwah, NJ: Paulist Press, 1982), 14.

7 See St. Francis, "A Mirror of the Perfection, *Rule*, Profession, Life, and True Calling of a Lesser Brother," in *Francis of Assisi: Early Documents*, vol. 3, *The Prophet*, 85.

8 These four would be Francis' closest companions and are today buried around him in the crypt of the Basilica of St. Francis.

Within the community, the brothers made known their needs to one another and they cared for each other as members of a family.[9] They consoled one another when they were hurting or suffering. They also challenged one another to strive for greater things. In community with others who were sincerely seeking God, the brothers helped each other see things about themselves that they could not necessarily see alone.

Their experience of community was the antithesis of individualism, and the fraternity would serve to counter the self-centered life constantly in search of personal well-being. Each brother's sense of responsibility and fraternal relationship toward those around him diminished his former life, in which he had been in search of self-aggrandizement through knighthood and personal glories. Previously, Francis often perceived others as a burden or a hindrance to achieving his will, and he often treated others as objects. However, in community, his companions were now brothers with whom he would share himself and his gifts—both material and otherwise.

Certainly community was at times difficult, and dealing with the fellow brothers could be one of the most challenging parts of their way of life. The brothers were no longer on their own time; they had to be respectful of one another, they had to be patient with one another, they had to put up with each other's sometimes challenging personalities. However, it was precisely in learning to love a "difficult" brother that they could find one of the best ways to learn charity.

---

9 See St. Francis, "The Later Rule," in *Francis and Clare: The Complete Works*, chap. 6.

For Francis, the day-to-day life of the community would be administered in a way that was "fraternal." No one would rule over or govern the community. Instead of having an abbot or prior, the leaders of the communities would be called simply guardians who would lead based on service, not rank.

The brothers chosen for leadership would not be "superior" to the others; rather, all would be lesser brothers.[10] They would make themselves "lesser" through humility and service. It did not matter if a brother had once been a nobleman or a commoner before entering; within the community, all were equal brothers.

The brothers were no longer bound to those strict social structures that had separated them in their former lives. Though the first four friars came from very different social backgrounds—Bernard the nobleman, Peter the jurist-canon, Francis the merchant, and Giles the peasant—they now lived as equal brothers. Their fraternal life based on humility, poverty, and penance smashed the social norms of the day, and their religious way of life would have been impossible in their previous lives in the "world." It leveled that feudal way of life based on vertical or hierarchical status—nobility with privileged birthrights, middle-class merchants, lowborn peasants, and the ecclesiastical canons with their own privileges.

Even within the Benedictine monasteries and convents, monks and nuns lived separately depending on their status. Those from noble backgrounds entered as privileged

---

10 See St. Francis, "The Earlier Rule," in *Francis and Clare: The Complete Works*, chap. 6, 3.

choristi who chanted the Divine Office in Latin. On the other hand, commoners from "lowborn" families entered as *conversi* and carried out most of the manual labor, since they could not read. They prayed by reciting *Pater Nosters* and *Ave Marias*. There was little interaction between the two groups. Ruling over all were the powerful abbots and abbesses.

Instead, the new life of the friars was horizontal. And together they went to the lowest place possible in society, the leper hospitals, to serve the outcasts who had no place at all in society.

The first friars would always know Rivotorto as the place where their community was conceived and grew up. For them, it was like a honeymoon after their recent marriage to Lady Poverty. Despite the hot Mediterranean summer sun, those biting winter winds, and the deluging spring rains, they were happy and joyful. They were in love.

They had uncluttered and simple spirits, and they felt truly free for the first time in their lives. Thomas described their life together with expressions such as "chaste embraces, gentle feelings, a holy kiss, pleasing conversation, modest laughter, joyous looks, a single eye, a submissive spirit, a peaceable tongue, a mild answer, oneness of purpose, ready obedience, unwearied hand."[11]

In a way that was familial and intimate, the early community at Rivotorto emulated the first Christian communities of the early Church. The brothers could say with

---

11 Thomas of Celano, "The Life of Saint Francis," in *Francis of Assisi: Early Documents*, ed. and trans. Regis J. Armstrong, vol. 1, *The Saint* (Hyde Park, NY: New City Press, 1999), chap. 15, 41.

Scripture: "Now the company of those who believed were of one heart and soul, and no one said that any of the things which he possessed was his own, but they had everything in common" (Acts 4:32). Ultimately, the earthly community that the brothers were establishing was a reflection of the kingdom of heaven.

Within the fraternity of Rivotorto, the brothers experienced peace, joy, charity, and love. It gave them more faith and hope. It was a foretaste of what they could hope for when one day they would be fully united with the communion of saints in the heavenly and mystical body of Christ.

Now Francis clearly understood the prophecy that he would become a great prince as well as the dream he had before departing for Spoleto—the one he had originally misinterpreted as a call to arms. It had told him that many knights would follow him and that he would be lord of a magnificent castle filled with arms and glorious shields. He had indeed become a knight among knights, fighting for their Lord and espoused to Lady Poverty. Rivotorto was their mansion, the cross their weapon, Scriptures their song.

But perhaps it was their unmitigated joy that made them the perfect knights of chivalry and courtesy. Francis had indeed become a great prince, a knight. The prophecy was true.

As more and more men from important Assisi families continued to leave everything and follow Francis, the townspeople became concerned. The most promising and important young men seemed to be throwing their lives away to embrace poverty. Also, when they went through towns preaching and serving the poor, people asked if they were orthodox or not.

Did they have permission from the bishop to preach? Were they part of the universal Catholic Church? Or were they on their own?

Francis and the brothers just answered, "We are penitents from the town of Assisi."[12] Eventually, however, their response would no longer be sufficient. They needed some form of credentials to clarify what they stood for.

---

12 "Three Companions," chap. 10, 37.

12

TO ROME

So then you are no longer strangers and sojourners, but
you are fellow citizens with the saints and members of the
household of God, built upon the foundation of the apostles
and prophets, Christ Jesus himself being the cornerstone.

EPHESIANS 2:19–20

IN the year 1209, when the brothers were twelve, they
realized they would need some kind of recognition or
authorization to continue living the way they were. They
were misunderstood too often. Therefore, Francis and the
brothers set out to Rome, hoping for an endorsement from
none other than Pope Innocent III.

Yet this action was not without risk, and the brothers
needed to proceed wisely. The Church authorities of the
day were traditionalists who valued time-tested forms of
life that were rooted in stability. It would be an understate-
ment to say that they were skeptical of novelties.

Pope Innocent III was one of the most powerful pon-
tiffs of the Middle Ages. He descended from the house of
Conti, which produced a total of nine popes. Politically, he
believed in a universal theocracy—that kings and their subjects alike throughout all of Christendom should be vassals
and subjects of an imperial papacy. Innocent was successful

as a statesman and diplomat who indeed expanded papal territories in central Italy as well as the power of the Church throughout Europe.

Of particular concern to Pope Innocent were the heterodox and heretical lay movements that were then quite diffused throughout Italy and the rest of Europe. The dissident groups came about after the Gregorian reforms of the mid-eleventh century, which were initiated to restore the moral integrity of the clergy, increase central authority within the Church, and reduce the influence of the emperor from ecclesial affairs.

However, perhaps unintentionally, it also initiated a religious revival among the laity. Scores of ordinary Christians longed for a return to the simplicity of the early Church described in the Gospels. In what was known as the *Vita Evangelica* (the Gospel life), simple, well-intentioned lay faithful rejected wealth, embraced material poverty, and preached the gospel itinerantly to anyone who would listen.

However, many of them began criticizing clerical worldliness, ecclesial opulence, and the feudal structure of the bishoprics and abbeys. Some groups like the Humiliati and Waldensians began orthodox, but after disobeying ecclesial directives, they ended up in schism and were excommunicated. More troublesome were the Cathars, sometimes referred to as Albigensians. After denunciations and excommunications, an exasperated Pope Innocent III launched a military campaign to eliminate Catharism in the south of France, Languedoc. His crusade took place the same year as Francis' visit in 1209.

Given the context, certainly Pope Innocent III would have found it difficult to endorse Francis and his group of poor friars. Quite frankly, they looked a lot like the heretics. How could he endorse these laypersons with no training to preach and evangelize?

Yet it was worth the risk for Francis and the brothers. Approval for their way of life directly from the Holy Father would be respected anywhere in Christendom and would leave no doubts as to what Francis and the brothers stood for. Francis was thoroughly Catholic—a *Vir Catholicus* (Catholic man), as the ancient legends referred to him— and his meeting with the pontiff was not political machination. Francis would never have dared preach against the Church he loved so dearly. His movement had to be part of and remain within the Church.

With a brief Rule in hand, composed mostly of Scripture verses, Francis and the brothers arrived in Rome with hope and trust in the Lord. Providentially, their own Bishop of Assisi, Guido, happened to be in Rome on business. With the recommendation of a cardinal who was fond of the Assisian bishop, the Holy Father agreed to meet the brothers at his papal residence next to the cathedral of Rome, St. John Lateran.

However, as soon as he saw them, the pope, who had more important matters at hand, promptly dismissed Francis and his motley group of ragamuffin penitents. "Go back to your pigsty," the pope said, ridiculing the friars. Francis, an extremist in so many things religious, obeyed the orders of the pope literally. They immediately left the opulent palace, exited the Roman city walls, and lay down with the pigs for the night at the first farm they came to.[1]

---

1 The original biographies do not indicate such harsh initial treatment during the friars' first audience with Pope Innocent. The pigsty version comes from Matthew of Paris.

However, that night, Pope Innocent had a dream that would forever change the direction of the Church. He saw the façade of the cathedral begin to lean, threatening to collapse.[2] Suddenly, a poor beggar appeared to the pontiff and, with arms outstretched, held the basilica up, preventing it from falling.

Pope Innocent awoke startled. He knew immediately that the man was Francis. He quickly called his guards and ordered them to find Francis and bring him back.

The poor brothers returned to the opulent papal palace. Francis knelt down on the Cosmatesque mosaic floor and lowered his head in deference to the highest authority in Christendom, the successor of Peter. Surrounded by his curia of prelates and cardinals with his jewel-encrusted papal tiara, the Vicar of Christ[3] was seated majestically on his elaborate papal cathedra. He was underneath an elevated baldacchino canopy supported by porphyry columns adorned with precious stones and cornices of gold and silver. He was high above everyone else in the chamber.

"What do you ask of us?" the Holy Father queried the poor penitent.

"The brothers and I wish to live poorly, to practice penance, and to preach the gospel of Jesus Christ. I want no other privilege than that of poverty. This is what I want."

Pope Innocent replied in a matter-of-fact way that Francis' understanding of literal poverty seemed too severe. The Holy Father said to Francis, "It seems to me that your

---

2 See Bonaventure of Bagnoregio, "The Major Legend of Saint Francis," in *Francis of Assisi: Early Documents*, ed. and trans. Regis J. Armstrong, vol. 2, *The Founder* (Hyde Park, NY: New City Press, 2000), chap. 3, 9.

3 Pope Innocent III was the first pope to use the title Vicar of Christ.

life of not having or possessing anything in this world is too rough and harsh. It is not practical.

"The twelve of you may be able to live your way of life in such extreme conditions now while you are young. But you will not be healthy and strong forever. What will happen when you get old and sick? Then, will those who come after you have the same zeal and fervor as you?

"Why don't you live under the Benedictine Rule? It is eight centuries old. It is time-tested. It allows for possessions. It is a concrete and holy way to live the Christian life together."

But Francis had to refuse. "Lord, if we had possessions, to defend them we would need arms. Or we would be forced to have recourse to law tribunals. We wish to avoid disputes and lawsuits that would impede love of God and neighbor. Therefore, we do not wish to possess anything of temporal value in this world."[4]

The pontiff continued with another practical consideration: "Why should I allow you—a layperson not living under a formal Rule, with no training, no ordination, and no mandate—to be allowed to preach in churches? You are a layperson, yet you admit priests into your movement who give their obedience to you. What authority do you have, poor Francis of Assisi?"

The pauper responded, "I have had but one guide: the Holy Gospel. After the Lord gave me brothers, no one

---

4 Cf. St. Francis, "The Beginning or the Founding of the Order and the Deeds of Those Lesser Brothers Who Were the First Companions of the Blessed Francis in Religion," in *Francis of Assisi: Early Documents*, vol. 2, *The Founder*, chap. 3, 17. Here, Francis counters the Bishop of Assisi with the above-cited words.

showed me what I should do but the Most High himself. Our Lord revealed to me that I should live according to the form of the Holy Gospel in poverty. The Holy Spirit as revealed in the Gospel has been my only guide.[5] We live a life of poverty and penance. This is what we wish to preach to the people."

Pope Innocent continued his interrogation. He was attempting to discern whether Francis was orthodox. "If the Holy Spirit is your only guide, then do you believe, like the heretics, that we are illegitimate? That we are not proper guides? That we are not following the gospel? That we do not represent the true Church of our Lord, Jesus Christ, and have fallen away?"

"No, Holy Father. To me, your will is the will of Christ," responded Francis. "Christ, our Lord, appointed Peter to lead his Church; the will of Peter is my will. The brothers and I will remain within the Barque of Peter.

"Whatever you command, I will do. I promise obedience and reverence to Your Holiness, the Pope, and to your successors and to the Church of Rome.[6] This is why we have come to Rome."

The Bishop of Rome did not let up. "Like you, the heretics embrace evangelical poverty. They are laypersons who preach; they claim inspiration directly from the Holy Spirit and Scripture. But they are not subject to any clerical control and they are turning many of the faithful

---

5 St. Francis, "The Testament," in *Francis and Clare: The Complete Works*, trans. Regis J. Armstrong (Mahwah, NJ: Paulist Press, 1982), 14. These were Francis' own words.

6 In Francis' Earlier Rule of 1221 (not approved) and Later Rule of 1223 (approved), Francis promises obedience to the pope.

against us. Tell me, Francis, which side do you choose? Are you and your followers heterodox or orthodox?"

Francis was unequivocal in stating his allegiance to the Bishop of Rome and to the Catholic Church. "All the brothers must be Catholics, and live and speak in a Catholic manner. If any should stray from the Catholic faith, in word or in deed, and has not amended his ways, he will be expelled from our brotherhood."[7]

Francis continued, "I, Brother Francis, and whoever will be the head of this Order, promise obedience and reverence to you, the Lord Pope Innocent, and to your successors. And all the other brothers will be bound to obey me and my successors."[8]

The pontiff seemed satisfied. Then he continued, "Then what do you ask from us? Do you wish us to make you a cleric? A priest, a bishop, or even a cardinal?"

"No. I am unworthy to become a priest or a canon. Instead, I wish to serve priests," responded Francis.

"None of us can ever be worthy of being an *Alter Christus*, my son," replied the pontiff. "Clerical ordination is a gift, not something we can ever merit." The Holy Father then asked Francis again if he was against the clerics.

"No. My wish is to be a lesser lay brother only," reiterated the humble friar. "Lord, we wish to be *minores*

---

7 These are Francis' exact words in "The Earlier Rule," in *Francis and Clare: The Complete Works*, chap. 19.

8 This is from the first line of Francis' Earlier Rule of 1221. In the Later Rule of 1223 (also known as the *Regula bullata*), Francis repeated himself, "Brother Francis promises obedience and reverence to the Lord Pope Honorius and his canonically elected successors and to the Roman Church. And let the other brothers be bound to obey Brother Francis and his successors."

(lessers) so that in no way will we presume to become *majores* (superiors). Our vocation is to remain humble and to follow in the footsteps of Christ's humility.

"We wish to be last in the eyes of men but first in the eyes of the saints. I wish to be lesser than you and the order of clerics, whom I esteem greatly. I wish to serve priests as my lords."

The pope then asked Francis what he believed about the Eucharist. "Do you believe—like the Waldensians—that sacraments given by unworthy and sinful priests are not valid? Or do you believe—like the Cathars—that any layman who believes in Christ and leads an exemplary, Christlike life may consecrate the sacrament of the altar? If you are not ordained a priest, will you, too, pretend to consecrate the Eucharist?"[9]

"I do not argue against holy orders," Francis replied. "For through the priest's hands—and only the priest's hands—do we receive the Holy Eucharist. And I believe this since I see nothing corporally of the Most High Son of God in this world except his most holy Body and Blood which priests receive and which they alone administer to others."[10]

Francis continued his defense of the priesthood: "For inasmuch as the priestly ministry is greater in that it concerns the most holy Body and Blood of our Lord Jesus Christ, which they receive and which they alone administer to others, so

---

9 Pope Innocent III would launch the Fourth Lateran Council in 1215 in an attempt to address the heresies that these groups were promoting, in addition to reforming Eucharistic practice, respecting churches and vessels, and reforming the clergy (among other things).

10 Francis, "Testament," 10.

those who sin against them commit a greater sin than if they sinned against all other people of this world."[11]

Francis continued praising priests: "The Lord gave me and still gives me such faith in priests who live according to the manner of the holy Roman Church because of their Order, that if they were to persecute me, I would still have recourse to them. And if I possessed as much wisdom as Solomon had and I came upon pitiful priests of this world, I would not preach contrary to their will in the parishes in which they live. And I desire to fear, love, and honor them and all others as my masters. And I do not wish to consider sin in them because I discern the Son of God in them and they are my masters."[12]

Francis went on: "Yet if I were to become a monk or a cleric, I would enter into a hierarchical tradition with fixed ways and expectations of how things are done. I would enter a community that was structured, ordered, well off, and privileged.

"I am called to the *Vita Evangelica*, the Gospel Life of total poverty. I always wish to submit to the clerical hierarchy as a loyal son of the Church. Yet I do not wish for myself or the brothers to be recipients of the dignity and respect that the clergy deserve."

The Holy Father then changed direction. "Do you believe, then, that we possess too much? That we are too rich? This is what the heretics say." This last question caught the attention

---

11 St. Francis, "The Admonitions," in *Francis and Clare: The Complete Works*, chap. 26.

12 Francis, "Testament," 6–9.

of several silk-clad cardinals seated near the pope. They leaned forward, listening attentively to Francis' response.

Francis responded, "I do not wish ecclesial privileges for myself not because wealth is sinful but because Christ called me to poverty through the words of Scripture."

"Then we are not living according to the Holy Gospel?" asked Innocent once again.

"Holy Father, I can say only what the Lord called me to do. I do not speak for anyone else." Francis became passionate now as he spoke. He moved around, gesticulating with his arms.

"Together with my first brothers, Scripture showed us to give away everything we had: 'If you would be perfect, go, sell what you possess and give to the poor, and you will have treasure in heaven; and come, follow me' (Mt 19:21); 'Take nothing for your journey' (Lk 9:3); and 'If any man would come after me, let him deny himself and take up his cross daily and follow me' (Lk 9:23). This is what we have sought to do. This is how we wish to live—according to the words of Jesus Christ himself."

Francis continued, "We wish to be humble because our Savior emptied himself of the divine glories of heaven. Scripture says 'he humbled himself' (Phil 2:8) as when the 'all-powerful word leaped from heaven, from the royal throne' (Wis 18:15) into the womb of the Virgin. Daily he comes to us in a humble form; daily he comes down from the 'bosom of the Father' (Jn 1:18) upon the altar in the hands of the priest."[13]

---

13 See Francis, "Admonitions," 14.

Pope Innocent was visibly moved by the poor man's words.

The saint continued as if singing: "Who are we that the God of the universe looks down at us and moves down to be with humanity—his creation—because of love? Christ came into the world born to poor parents. Joseph was a carpenter who worked with his hands.

"Working with one's hands is something the commoners do, not the nobility. Jesus associated with the marginalized—lepers, tax collectors, and outcasts. Finally, our Lord went to the cross to die as a convicted criminal— the lowliest place possible—the cross.

"We, too, wish to live like our Savior, Jesus the Christ, who was humble. Scripture says, 'Learn from me; for I am gentle and lowly in heart' (Mt 11:29). I was once rich, but I emptied myself of all earthly glories, honors, privileges, and wealth. I once sought to be a wealthy merchant, a knight, a nobleman, and an important citizen of Assisi. Yet now I choose poverty like Christ. I lowered myself to live as a mendicant. I have placed myself at the service of the lowliest of society, the leper. My brothers do the same as I.

"It is our wish only to be humble, minor, lesser brothers. We wish to be humble by being charitable to one other, by loving lowliness, by being a brother to everybody. We wish to be subject to all as true lesser brothers. We do not deserve the honors of being a lord bishop; we wish to be subject to you. I wish this fraternity to be called the Order of *Fratres Minores* [Friars Minor]. It is my most humble desire that you will confirm our life for us."

With that, Francis told a story.[14] "Once upon a time, there was a poor but lovely woman who lived in the desert. The king came and fell in love with her because of her incomparable beauty and made her his wife. With her, he had many handsome children.

"When they had grown up and been nobly educated, their mother said, 'Dear children, do not be ashamed because you are poor, for you are all children of a great king. Go joyfully to his court and ask for whatever you need.'

"They went and presented themselves to the king. They were not afraid to look at him, since they bore his very image. When the king saw his image within them, he was surprised, and he asked them whose sons they might be. When they said they were the children of the poor woman who lived in the desert, the king embraced them, saying, 'You are my heirs and my sons. Have no fear!' The king then sent orders to the woman to send all his sons to be fed at his court."

Then Francis bowed in respect and homage to the successor of Peter in full submission to the Holy Father's will.

Pope Innocent closed his eyes for a moment, appearing lost in thought. He understood that Francis was the woman who bore many children—the friars. The desert was the world—wild and barren, lacking in virtue. The king was the Son of God, whom they resembled by their holy poverty.

The pauper's words stirred something buried deep within him, seemingly forgotten long ago. Francis reminded Innocent of his own ideas and writings many years earlier, before becoming pope. He had once written a treatise on

---

14 See Thomas of Celano, "The Remembrance of the Desire of a Soul," in *Francis of Assisi: Early Documents*, vol. 2, *The Founder*, chap. 11, 16.

poverty called *De Contemptu Mundi*, in which he wrote how Christians should hold worldly matters in contempt.

Innocent III was not a corrupt pope; he had the heart of a pastor. Pope Innocent believed in Francis. He felt like a father—a grandfather even—to the young man in front of him.

The Holy Father opened his eyes and declared to Francis, the friars, and all his curia: "We give you permission to live the life in the way you have presented it to us, in accordance with the Holy Scriptures. We will now give you and your brothers the tonsure, which will impart to you Church authority and will prevent accusations of heresy.

"We will ordain you, Francis, a deacon, granting you clerical authority to preach in churches.[15] Remember always to preach and teach according to the doctrine of the Holy Roman Church. From now on, your movement will be the Ordo Fratrum Minorum—the Order of Lesser Brothers."

The Holy Father told Francis that his secretary would prepare the necessary documents, stating everything he had approved. But Francis refused, saying, "Holy Father, your word is enough for me." Filled with joy, he and the brothers kissed the ring of the pontiff and set back out to Assisi, content to have the Holy Father's oral approval to live their way of life.

As the pope and his curia watched Francis and the brothers leave, a skeptical cardinal leaned forward and asked the Holy Father, "Do you think he will become another

---

15 It is mere speculation that Francis was ordained a deacon here. No one knows precisely when he was ordained a deacon.

Waldo of Lyons[16] or, worse, will embrace the Catharist heresies?"

Innocent responded, "No. I know that Francis will do great things for the Church. Through his Order, he will renew the Church."

The encounter between Francis and Innocent was momentous. Francis—a relatively insignificant, highly charismatic, voluntary pauper who had only recently come to believe in and trust the promptings of the Holy Spirit as his only guide—met Pope Innocent III, an ecclesiastical bureaucrat who ruled over the powerful Catholic Church from a throne of opulence. Francis believed that the Holy Spirit was guiding him and would never fail him or his movement; for him, the Holy Spirit inflamed him to follow in the footprints of Jesus Christ.[17] The pope believed in and worked within the institutional structures of the Holy See.

Yet between the two of them, charism and institution were not polemical or inherently conflicted; rather, they

---

16 Waldo of Lyons, also known as Peter Waldo, was born around 1140 in Lyons, France. He had been a wealthy merchant, but after a conversion around the age of twenty, he gave away his riches to the poor. After he gained followers, he went to Rome in 1179 seeking permission from Pope Alexander III to live his way of life. They were never given full permission to openly preach and were eventually excommunicated. The Waldensian sect still survives to this day, predominantly in parts of northern Italy and southern France.

17 Francis' prayer that he offered for his friars in *A Letter to the Entire Order* expresses his trust in the Holy Spirit well: "Almighty, eternal, just and merciful God, grant us in our misery the grace to do for You alone what we know You want us to do, and always to desire what pleases You. Thus, inwardly cleansed, interiorly enlightened, and inflamed by the fire of the Holy Spirit, may we be able to follow in the footprints of Your beloved Son, our Lord Jesus Christ."

joined hands in complementarity and mutuality to rebuild the Church together.[18] Francis placed his movement within the hands of the institutional Church, in which he steadfastly believed, to draw on its support, wisdom, and experience so that it could grow and flourish. The pope, aware that the institutional Church could not live solely by rules, regulations, and administration without eventually tiring and dying, embraced the charisma, freshness, vitality, and inspiration that Francis brought.

In acts of humility, Francis and Pope Innocent both recognized that charism and institution were always complementary components of the Church. Together they brought spirit and structure, inspiration and organization, anima and animus. Francis and Innocent were both able to look beyond their own gifts in order to rebuild the Church together.

Francis' fledgling group of penitents had now emerged from the loose penitential movement as an established, recognized, and distinct Order of the Church, the Order of Friars Minor. It was April 16, the day that constitutes the official founding of the Franciscan Order. On that day, Francis established his minor movement within the official canonical structure of the One, Holy, Catholic, and Apostolic Church.

The friars left Rome rejoicing in the goodness of the Lord. On their way back to Assisi, the brothers stayed for a few months in the area of Narni, near Terni in lower

---

18 Pope Benedict XVI described the institution of the Church under Innocent III and the charism of Francis in such terms as "complementary" and "mutual" when he addressed the friars gathered in Assisi in 2009 for the second Chapter of Mats.

Umbria, where they served the poor. After returning to Rivotorto, they were surprised to discover a surly farmer who had moved his donkeys into their sheds.

Instead of contesting the peasant, the friars left. They desired to move their humble residence to St. Mary of the Angels. The Benedictine monks of San Benedetto[19] on Mount Subasio owned the property, so Francis and the brothers went to the abbot of the monastery to ask his permission. He agreed. In exchange, the brothers offered the monks a basket of fish.

---

19 The monastery of San Benedetto still exists. It is about one mile from the Carceri. Today it is mostly ruined, although there have been various projects to restore it.

13

PRAYING IN THE HERMITAGE

*But when you pray, go into your room and shut the door
and pray to your Father who is in secret; and your Father
who sees in secret will reward you.*

MATTHEW 6:6

F RANCIS loved the mountains. They brought him close
to God. And his native country is full of them, from
the Alps in the north to the Apennines that run all the way
down the peninsula.

He spent his life constantly climbing up mountains
and then descending back down to the valleys. His hardy
ruggedness came out while climbing those steep, windy
switchbacks up the harsh, craggy peaks and through the
thick oak forests. But his masculine vigor was balanced by
the tender emotions he felt while admiring the serene landscape below. The cool mountain air; the forests wooded
with poplar, holm oaks, maple, and beech trees; fresh
snow; mountain streams; the fragrance of wild mint, lilies,
and roses all filled his soul and drew him closer to heaven.

On the peaks, he praised God and felt connected to the
great prophets such as Moses on Sinai and Elijah on Carmel.
He would search out places of retreat among the crags and
caves where he could be alone and pray. After long periods

of time in deep prayer among the mountains, Francis would emerge transformed, almost like Jesus on Mount Tabor.

When Francis gazed up toward the sky from the mountaintops, his eyes were raised and his soul lifted up. The mountains pointed the way to God: up. In ancient times, mountains were considered the seats of the gods, as the mountains were "up high" and closer to the heavens.

On the mountaintop, Francis worshipped God alone: "Hear, O Israel: The LORD our God is one LORD; and you shall love the LORD your God with all your heart, and with all your soul, and with all your might" (Dt 6:4–5). There on high, God revealed himself as a God who was sacred, creator, lawgiver, mysterious, incomprehensible, omniscient, almighty, imposing, and omnipotent.

On the mountains, God showed himself to be the one transcendent God. God before the world, above the world, outside of the world. The mountains would always stand as a reminder to Francis that his gaze, his mind, and his heart should not rest only on the horizon of this world, on its material things, but that they be directed toward God. The mountains were like the vertical part of the cross, the part that pointed up to God.

While Francis descended from the mountains to the valley below, he considered the other aspect of Christian spirituality: immanence. The cross had two beams—vertical as well as horizontal. Down in the valley, Francis would live out the horizontal imperative to serve others.

The valley was like the Incarnation—how Christ humbled and lowered himself from the heavens above to be with humanity down below. God reached down, stooped down, from heaven to be with us. God did not stay hidden;

he became a child. He did not hide from humanity; he revealed himself as a man.

In his incarnation, God became close to man and allowed for relationship and unity in the material world. Thus Francis—like Christ—would always have a strong concern for the world. He would always desire to help the poor and the marginalized, he would focus on being together in community and fellowship, he believed strongly in the individual conscience. For Francis, God was not just an all-powerful "being" up in heaven somewhere; he was with us here where we are—God is immanent, God is love.

For Francis, the entire spiritual life would be like walking up and down mountains. Going up: being with the transcendent God in prayer and hermitage to receive strength. This would give him the strength to work in the world. Going down: being down in the valley to serve the lepers and preach in the cities.

Francis' life would not be prayer alone or ministry alone; it would be both prayer and ministry, alternating between the mountains and the plains. It would be both transcendent and immanent. Francis' mountains would be both Mount Sinai and the Mount of Beatitudes. Never the first or the second, but both—one in fulfillment of the other.

Francis frequently chose solitary places in the mountains where he could direct his mind completely to God. There in the clefts of the rock he would build his nest, and in the hollow places of the wall, his dwelling.[1] The hermitages

---

1 See Thomas of Celano, "The Life of Saint Francis," in *Francis of Assisi: Early Documents*, ed. and trans. Regis J. Armstrong, vol. 1, *The Saint* (Hyde Park, NY: New City Press, 1999), chap. 27.

were always up in the hills and mountains, away from the towns or cities. They were simple, austere, and poor places of prayer.

They were not monasteries made of thick, stone walls, denoting *stabilitas*—permanency and strength. Instead, they were temporary, simple, unpretentious, natural structures. They were devoid of fine art, icons, furnishings, and decorations; yet they were elegant, as they were immersed in the setting of nature. For Francis, they were the perfect place to pray and fast.

In his life, Francis founded some twenty mountain hermitages throughout all of Italy.[2] Closer to Assisi was a hermitage known in Francis' era as the *Sasso del Maloloco*, located some 1,200 feet above the city.[3] Today it is called

---

2 Hermitages founded or visited by Francis that still have active communities today are Laverna and the Cells of Cortona in Tuscany; Monteluco, Montecasale, and Monteripido in Umbria; Greccio, Poggio Bustone, La Foresta, and Fonte Colombo in Lazio; and Valleremita, San Liberato, and Brugliano in the Marches.

3 Nestled in the forest on Mount Subasio at 2,600 feet above sea level, the Carceri is a peaceful setting for solitude and prayer. As you enter, on the left you will notice a friary erected by St. Bernardine of Siena in the fifteenth century. You can enter and visit the refectory, dormitory, and oratory. Continuing into the hermitage, you will pass by the chapel dedicated to St. Bernardine. Then you will descend some windy, narrow stairs and come upon a space carved into the cliff where Francis slept. This is the oldest part of the hermitage. Emerging from the sanctuary, you will discover a wonderful natural setting among the forest of ilex trees (a type of oak) with a long footpath and several outdoor altars. Notice an ancient braced holm oak tree where, according to tradition, Francis blessed some birds perching on its branches. You will see some bronze sculptures by the Italian artist, Fiorenzo Bacci, of Francis, Leo, and Giles. They are gazing at the stars, each responding according to his personality and education. Further along on the right are several trails steeply descending to various caves named

the Carceri, which means "prisons" or "cells." Like St. Paul, Francis became a "prisoner of Christ" (cf. Eph 3:1).

The hermitage was made up of a series of rocks, crags, cliffs, and caves along a ravine on Mount Subasio. Owned by the Benedictine monks of San Benedetto not far away, penitents and monks had been withdrawing to these caves for prayer for many centuries.

In the poverty of the Carceri, Francis immersed himself in nature as God created it. He reveled in her simplicity. In the stillness of the hermitages, he listened to nature's sounds and watched her movements. He marveled at the chirping of the birds, the rustling of the leaves in the wind, the dancing insects.

As Francis lay in the open outdoors at night, he wondered at the majesty of the stars. During the cold months, the heat of the fire warmed his body and his inner being; he always kept the embers lit as long as possible. How he rejoiced on those first spring days when the power of the Mediterranean sun warmed the land on which he often lay. During the hot summer months, the coolness of the caves refreshed his body.

As Francis descended into the barrenness of the caves in solitude and silence, he felt like he was entering into something much bigger than himself. It was almost as if he were descending into the womb of the earth where he felt God comforting, nurturing, and protecting him. In the caves, he was filled with a powerful—almost overwhelming—sense of God's power, goodness, and love.

---

after the first friars. Today, the Carceri is used as a hermitage by the O.F.M. friars. It has a small guesthouse for retreatants.

At the same time, there was something about the cracks in the rock that reminded Francis of brokenness. Yet even there he felt Christ's presence. When he would walk down along the bottom of the ravine of the *fosso*, or ditch, it was truly the *fosso del diavolo*, "the pit of the Devil." There all the refuse of the mountain gathered—dead trees, rocks, and boulders. The caves reminded him of the lepers. They reminded him of Christ.

Praying in the hermitage for Francis was to be temporary, never permanent. It was not a monastery. Prayer was his connection to God, and it gave him a source of energy to allow him to rededicate himself to the active life. Yet Francis loved the spirituality of the hermitages so much that, at times, he would feel tempted to stay there forever as a lifelong hermit.[4]

In this regard, he was similar to the Apostle Peter, who wished to build a tent and remain on Mount Tabor (see Mt 17:4). Yet Francis could not stay on the mountain forever; the full gospel life would call him to once again descend to the plains below to continue preaching and serving the poor. Francis was too much of an itinerant to have retired as a hermit.

Francis prayed deeply and profoundly in the hermitages. Some years, he would spend four or five forty-day fasts up in the hermitages—almost half the year. He prayed and fasted during three "Lents" in addition to the Lent preceding Easter, the feast of the Assumption to Michaelmas

---

4 See "The Little Flowers of Saint Francis," in *Francis of Assisi: Early Documents*, ed. and trans. Regis J. Armstrong, vol. 3, *The Prophet* (Hyde Park, NY: New City Press, 2001), chap. 16.

(August 15–September 29), the forty days preceding the Feast of Sts. Peter and Paul, and the forty days after the Epiphany.

When Francis prayed, he gave his entire self to God: his heart, soul, desire, joy, emotions, memory, and feelings. He would take everything—his thoughts, concerns, hopes, worries, troubles, sins—all that he was. He emptied himself of the things of the world in order to be completely filled by God and to become dependent on God. In prayer, Francis was like clay in the hands of the Potter; he was free to become the person that God made him to be.

In prayer, Francis sought to become one with his Creator. His way of praying involved his whole self, his complete animus, his entire being, his emotions. His biographer said, "His whole soul thirsted after Christ, and he dedicated not only his whole heart, but his whole body as well, to him."[5]

Francis felt God in his body, he tasted the sweetness of heaven on his tongue, and he saw visions of God and the angels. Whether he was walking or sitting, at home or abroad, working or resting, he was so fervently devoted to prayer that he seemed to have dedicated to it not only his heart and soul but all his efforts and time. He experienced God with his emotions and the world was tasteless to him who was fed with heavenly sweetness.[6]

In his prayer life, Francis was frequently practical, sensible, and natural. His spirituality was rooted in the human,

---

5 Thomas of Celano, "The Remembrance of the Desire of a Soul," in *Francis of Assisi: Early Documents*, ed. and trans. Regis J. Armstrong, vol. 2, *The Founder* (Hyde Park, NY: New City Press, 2000), chap. 61, 94.

6 See Bonaventure of Bagnoregio, "The Major Legend of Saint Francis," in *Francis of Assisi: Early Documents*, vol. 2, *The Founder*, chap. 10, 1.

earthly experience of Christ, and his prayer was incarnational. Although Francis frequently enjoyed great mystical experiences in prayer, in the end, he never sought to remain above or beyond the world. Prayer was not abstract, metaphysical, or transcendent—a *fuga mundi*. For Francis, prayer was modeled after the God who was not "up there" but had lowered himself by becoming a man in the world (cf. Phil 2:6–8).

He desired to enter into the humanity of Christ of the Gospel, personally and passionately. He sought to enter into that human-divine mystery by seeking to see, touch, feel, make present, and even visually reproduce the events of the human life of Christ—where he was born, lived, died, and was resurrected. Thus he often meditated on the historical, concrete stories from the life of Christ, such as his nativity, passion, and resurrection.

His first biographer said, "Francis used to recall with regular meditation the words of Christ and recollect his deeds with most attentive perception. Indeed, so thoroughly did the humility of the Incarnation and the charity of the Passion occupy his memory that he scarcely wanted to think of anything else."[7]

His biographer said of Francis while praying: "For his safest haven was prayer; not prayer of a single moment, or idle or presumptuous prayer, but prayer of long duration; full of devotion, serene in humility. If he began late, he would scarcely finish before morning. Walking, sitting, eating, or drinking, he was always intent upon prayer. He

---

7 Celano, "Life of Saint Francis," in *Francis of Assisi: Early Documents*, vol. 1, *The Saint*, chap. 30, 85.

would go alone to pray at night in churches abandoned and located in deserted places, where, under the protection of divine grace, he overcame many fears and many disturbances of mind."[8]

In the end, Francis' prayer was focused on the imitation of Christ. Like Jesus, Francis would leave his retreat and go back down to the valley to serve the lepers, the community, and the Church. Yet through prayer, Francis became more and more a channel of God's grace and love. He became more and more united to God.

His mind was so drawn away from worldly things that he enjoyed great peace in prayer. He was neither excited by worldly desires nor moved by the passions. His mind was constantly fixed on God and his attention turned frequently to him.

Thomas of Celano said of Francis, "Thus he would direct all his attention and affection toward the one thing he asked of the Lord, not so much praying as becoming totally prayer."[9] His biographer said that after praying, Francis was changed almost into another man[10]—another Christ.

---

8 Ibid., chap. 27, 71.

9 Celano, "Remembrance," in *Francis of Assisi: Early Documents*, vol. 2, *The Founder*, chap. 61, 95.

10 See Ibid., chap. 65, 99.

14

ON PILGRIMAGE

They were strangers and exiles on the earth.

HEBREWS 11:13

IT was 1217, and the first General Chapter of the Friars Minor had just been celebrated at St. Mary of the Angels. By now, the "fraternity" was made up of thousands of men. Francis decided to send them to all nations.

So they divided the known world into geographical districts, called provinces. The title "Mother Province of the Order" was assigned to the Holy Land, and Brother Elias of Cortona and several other friars were sent there to found it. Two years later in 1219, Francis himself would attempt to go on pilgrimage to visit the Holy Land Province.

There was nothing new about Christians going to the Holy Land, as they had been going there for many centuries. Since the fourth century when Emperor Constantine and his mother, Helena, built large churches and shrines in Palestine to memorialize events from the Gospels and Christ's life, they paved the way for countless Christians to come. Pilgrims who could not get that far stayed within Europe, going to Rome, Compostela, and Monte Sant'Angelo.

For Francis, the pilgrimage was the perfect way to live the Christian life. To be a pilgrim meant surrendering identity, class, and security. On the road, no one had status—all were basically equal.

Before setting off, the medieval pilgrim prepared a last will and testament, gave away or sold his possessions, and celebrated the Church's sending-off liturgical rite, which was similar to that of a funeral. After donning the recognizable pilgrim's tunic with a sewn-in cross, the walking staff, and leather pouch to carry food and money, the pilgrim set off on the journey. Symbols were important: those headed to the tomb of St. James in Compostela sowed an image of the scallop shell on their tunic; those going to Rome were called Romeos and wore keys; those going to the Holy Land took the Jerusalem cross.

The distinctive dress set the pilgrims apart and identified them as such for protection. Pilgrims traveled poorly, accepted alms, and depended on the kindness of others. By surrendering material things of the world and placing their trust and hope completely in God's providence, the pilgrim voluntarily embraced a state of insecurity and instability.

Their poverty and instability necessitated faith in God's Providence. Yet the dangers of disease, robbery, shipwrecks, and strife were real, and few returned home. For Francis, it was perfect.

To be a pilgrim was biblical. Abram set out on the first pilgrimage when he was called by God to leave his pagan past and his father's home in order to migrate to the Promised Land (see Gn 12:1–4). Later, Moses was called by God to leave Egypt with the Hebrew people (see Ex 12:37–19:8).

Abraham and Moses followed the voice of God, who led them forth on a journey. The journey involved a long period of struggle, uncertainty, doubt, and difficulty through the desert where, at times, they felt lost or confused. However, they ultimately arrived at a better place. They heard the voice, departed, and wandered as foreigners in exile, yet ultimately they arrived in a purified place and state.

Jesus' human life on earth can be compared to a pilgrimage as well. Like the Old Testament prophets, he too listened to the voice of his Father, obeyed, and left his "home" by becoming incarnate in the world. In this world as "sojourner," he too lived as a "pilgrim and stranger." As Abraham and Moses "wandered" through the desert, Jesus on earth "had nowhere to rest his head" (cf. Lk 9:58; Mt 8:20). His mission was to journey through the land of this fallen world in order to redeem it and its inhabitants. And like the prophets, Jesus ultimately went to a better place after his resurrection.

New Testament writers also used pilgrimage to describe the Christian life: become "strangers and exiles on the earth" (Heb 11:13); "I beseech you as aliens and exiles to abstain from the passions of the flesh that wage war against your soul" (1 Pt 2:11); "conduct yourselves with fear throughout the time of your exile" (1 Pt 1:17).

Francis modeled his entire life after pilgrimage. His pilgrimage began when he embraced Christ after rejecting the military life. He became a true "pilgrim and stranger" when he left the security of his father's home as a young man and embraced a way of instability and insecurity through poverty.

He often referred to pilgrimage in his writings: "Let the brothers not make anything their own, neither house, nor place, nor anything at all. As pilgrims and strangers in this world, serving the Lord in poverty and humility, let them go seeking alms with confidence."[1] "Let the brothers be careful not to receive in any way churches or poor dwellings or anything else built for them unless they are according to the holy poverty we have promised in the Rule. As pilgrims and strangers, let them always be guests there."[2] His biographers said of Francis and pilgrimage, "He always wanted the laws of pilgrims for his sons: to be sheltered under someone else's roof, to travel in peace, and to thirst for the homeland."[3] "He wanted everything to sing of exile and pilgrimage."[4] "They went through the world as strangers and pilgrims, taking nothing for the journey."[5]

For Francis, the goal of the pilgrimage was to encounter the living God. Therefore, pilgrimage was about going to particular "holy" or "sacred" places in order to receive special graces through the spirituality or sacredness of place. The pilgrimage was about going forth in the world, which was created good by God the Father through the

---

1 St. Francis, "The Later Rule," in *Francis and Clare: The Complete Works*, trans. Regis J. Armstrong (Mahwah, NJ: Paulist Press, 1982), chap. 6, 2.

2 St. Francis, "The Testament," in *Francis and Clare: The Complete Works*, 24.

3 Thomas of Celano, "The Remembrance of the Desire of a Soul," in *Francis of Assisi: Early Documents*, ed. and trans. Regis J. Armstrong, vol. 2, *The Founder* (Hyde Park, NY: New City Press, 2000), chap. 29.

4 "The Assisi Compilation," in *Francis of Assisi: Early Documents*, vol. 2, *The Founder*, 24.

5 "The Legend of the Three Companions," in *Francis of Assisi: Early Documents*, vol. 2, *The Founder*, chap. 14, v. 59; see also St. Francis, "The Beginning or the Founding of the Order and the Deeds of Those Lesser Brothers Who Were the First Companions of the Blessed Francis in Religion," in *Francis of Assisi: Early Documents*, vol. 2, *The Founder*, chap. 9, v. 40.

Word, sanctified by the Holy Spirit, and redeemed through the incarnation and crucifixion of the Son. The pilgrimage was a response within his soul to move outward to God; it required a departure from his ordinary life in order to embrace the unknown within the context of faith.

Since childhood, Francis had always longed to go to the Holy Land. When he was just five years old, Jerusalem fell to the Muslim army led by Saladin. All of Christendom felt the blow, and it rekindled in Christians of all backgrounds a desire to go and take Christ's land back for Christianity.

Before his conversion, Francis wanted to go to the Holy Land as a crusader. In fact, it was largely the stories told by the crusaders returning home from battle there that instilled in Francis a desire to go and fight. Yet after his conversion, when he laid down his sword and renounced the life as a crusader, he never lost that desire to walk in the footsteps of Christ in the sacred places of Jesus' earthly life. What better way to connect with the Lord than to go to the actual land of his earthly life?

So Francis went. He would join that long pilgrimage tradition of visiting the sites of his Savior's birthplace, crucifixion, and resurrection. Possessing nothing but faith in God and his desire to be a pilgrim, Francis set out for the Holy Land.[6] He and a brother boarded a ship in Italy bound for Syria.

Soon after setting sail, however, they were blown off course, landing in Dalmatia (present-day Croatia). But this

---

6 See Thomas of Celano, "The Life of Saint Francis," in *Francis of Assisi: Early Documents*, ed. and trans. Regis J. Armstrong, vol. 1, *The Saint* (Hyde Park, NY: New City Press, 1999), chap. 20.

still did not dampen his desire to continue the pilgrimage. After he realized that no ships were sailing to Syria that year from Dalmatia, he tried to get back to Italy, seeking passage with some sailors heading to Ancona, a port city on the Adriatic Sea. But since Francis had no money, they refused.

Trusting fully in the Lord, Francis sneaked on board with his companion. Providentially, another man came on board, bringing with him enough extra provisions for Francis and the other friar. After they set sail, a storm arose and once again blew the ship off course.

When the crew had gone through all their provisions, only those of the poor friars remained. The saintly brothers generously gave of their provisions to the crew. By God's grace, the food lasted until they reached the port of Ancona.

At this point, Francis decided against going by sea. On his second attempt, he would walk from Assisi all the way to Spain, cross the strait by ship, and arrive in North Africa in Morocco. Then he would continue to Jerusalem on foot.

So strong was his desire to reach his destination that at times he left his companion behind as if inebriated in spirit and enthusiasm to be in the Holy Land. Yet once again, it was not God's will. When he arrived in Spain, Francis was struck with an illness and was forced to turn back to Assisi once again. Perhaps he was well enough to visit the sanctuary of St. James in Compostela on the way.

His desire to walk in the footsteps of his Lord never left him, and he attempted to get there yet a third time. This time he was successful. However, his experience as a pilgrim in the Holy Land would not go as he planned. God had other ideas.

15

PEACE AND THE SULTAN

Peace I leave with you; my peace I give to you; not as the world gives do I give to you.

JOHN 14:27

IT was July 1219, and Francis set out to the Holy Land for his third and final attempt. This time he was successful. He arrived in St. John of Acre, the newly established capital city of the Latin Kingdom of the Holy Land.

In 1187, the crusaders had lost Jerusalem to the Muslim ruler, Saladin, and retreated to the north in Acre. There Francis met Brother Elias and the other friars who had arrived two years earlier to found the Holy Land Province. But they never got further than Acre.

They explained to Francis that it was now impossible to visit the Christian sites and walk in the footsteps of the Lord in Bethlehem, Nazareth, and Jerusalem. War was under way between Christians and Muslims. During times of truce it might be possible, but currently the Fifth Crusade was being fought.

As it had so many times before in his life, Francis felt the Spirit move him to do something wild. He would go to the Saracens, embrace the Muslim sultan, and preach the peace of Christ. He hoped the sultan would embrace

Christianity, and there would be peace between Christians and Muslims.

He knew it could lead to his martyrdom, but this did not frighten him. In fact, he desired it.

Francis promptly boarded the first ship for Damietta in Egypt, where a battle was raging. When Francis arrived at port, he saw flags flying from nations all over the Western world: France, Germany, Britain, Spain, and Holland. From Italy, there were ships from the Republics of Venice, Genoa, Pisa, Lucca, and Bologna. All had the same shield-shaped emblem: the crimson-colored crusader cross on a white background.

The Bishop of Acre, Jacques de Vitry, wrote of Francis' arrival: "We saw the arrival of the friar Francis, founder of the Order of Friars Minor. He was a simple and unlettered man, but most lovable and dear to God and to men. He arrived when the army of the Crusaders was encamped below Damietta; he was immediately respected by all."

Another bishop witnessed the arrival of Francis, too—Cardinal Pelagius. Pelagius was in Damietta with orders from Pope Honorius III to plan the battle of Damietta together with the crusader commander, John of Brienne. Francis knew of John, as he had once set out to fight for his brother, Walter, in that other crusade against the excommunicated emperor, Otto, in southern Italy. Ironically, that had been the moment when Francis had forever put down the crusader's sword and armor in Spoleto.

Having lost Jerusalem, the crusaders were now attempting to take Damietta, an important city on the Nile delta leading to Cairo, which they were hoping to exchange for

Jerusalem. However, things were not looking good for them. They were far outnumbered.

Many of the crusaders were a motley assortment of mercenaries, thugs, and thieves. They were there for money and the excitement of looting. Perhaps some were indeed repentant for past crimes and were seeking the plenary indulgence.

The cardinal and John were arguing over strategy. It appeared that Francis came at a good time. Yet Francis did not come to help his fellow Christians as a combatant. He was there for a different reason: peace. And his encounter with the sultan would change the course of history.

Francis asked the cardinal for permission to cross the lines to speak directly with the sultan. He would seek to bring peace. Pelagius, John, and the other military commanders looked at one another and laughed. "You want to speak with the Saracen infidels?" scoffed the cardinal. "They are uncivilized savages! They'll crucify you!"

John of Brienne was less kind in his assessment of the Saracens, and he summed up what the crusaders thought of the Islamic people: "The Muslims are a desert slave race. They are Asian pagans, children of the devil. They are worse than the most barbarous heathens you've ever encountered in Europe. If they are gentle with you, they will merely crucify you!"

Cardinal Pelagius tried to explain, "They are not Christians, my son. The Saracens are illegitimate descendants of Abraham through Sarah's slave girl, Hagar, and her illegitimate son, Ishmael.

"They are not the legitimate people of God of Abraham through Sarah and Isaac. We are. They are a cursed race. And now they are once again in control of Jerusalem.

"Not only are they forbidding Christian pilgrims from going to the holy sites of our Lord, Jesus Christ; they are destroying our churches. We must reconquer Jerusalem, reestablish a Latin Kingdom in the homeland of our Savior, and protect the holy Christian sites. *Deus Vult* (God wills it)."

The cardinal went on to explain to Francis the history of Jerusalem.

"My son, Jerusalem is very important to us. It was there where our Lord, Jesus Christ, was crucified and resurrected. In A.D. 70, just as Christ had prophesied, after the Jews revolted, the Romans destroyed their second temple.

"With Emperor Constantine's Edict of Milan in the year 313, and subsequent Christian Byzantine rule over the Holy Land, a period of great peace for Christians reigned. More than two hundred churches and monasteries were built throughout the Holy Land. Yet when the founder of their religion, Muhammad, was born in 570, things would go badly for us.

"Shortly thereafter, the Zoroastrian Persians invaded the Holy Land in 614 and destroyed many of our churches—including the Church of the Holy Sepulchre. They also carried away numerous relics to Persia, including the True Cross, the Holy Lance, and the Holy Sponge. The one bright spot was that they spared the Basilica of the Nativity because of the depiction in a mosaic of the Three Kings who were dressed like Assyrian Kings.

"Then, by the grace of God, Emperor Heraclius, a Christian Byzantine ruler, reconquered the Holy Land and reestablished Christian rule. But only for two decades. In 637, that Muslim Omar conquered Jerusalem and established

Arab rule. They murdered Christian pilgrims from the West and East and forbade all Christian worship.

"Finally, in 1095, Pope Urban II called for the first holy war—a crusade—to help our Christian brothers in the East against the onslaught and to reestablish a Latin Kingdom in Jerusalem. And in 1099 we were successful in once again reestablishing a Christian kingdom in Jerusalem.

"We built roads, castles, and fortifications. We also rebuilt our churches, thus guaranteeing Christians the possibility of safe pilgrimage. However, in 1187, Saladin defeated us and took Jerusalem back once again for the Muslims.

"That was a day of mourning for Christians throughout all of Christendom. People throughout Europe went about in mourning and dressed in sackcloth. Everyone in Europe spoke only of Jerusalem and of restoring the welfare of the faith and the glory of God. We had to take back the Holy Sepulchre for Christ. Finally, in the Lateran Council, Pope Innocent promoted another crusade—the fifth one. And now we are here—to take it back."

Francis understood well the reason the crusaders were there. He was present at the Fourth Lateran Council of 1215 and had heard Pope Innocent's passionate call to arms. Yet Francis did not support war or violence. He had renounced it long before in Spoleto while seeking knighthood by fighting on behalf of no less than John's own brother, Walter of Brienne.

For Francis, it mattered not whether the Crusades were waged against Saracens, excommunicated emperors, or heretical Cathars. Francis had long ago put down his sword (cf. Mt 26:52), which he turned into a plowshare (cf. Is 2:4). He was now a man of peace.

On the way to the battlefield that second time in Spoleto, Francis' life was forever changed. His eyes were opened that night as he began to understand something about peace. The question the Lord posed to him that night, "Who are you serving?," haunted him. He was forced to search deep within and discover that the source of his conflict was not external; instead, Francis' true war was internal.

He had longed to become a knight for personal glory and honor. People were objects that either helped him advance his agenda or stood in his way. He had been ready to raise the sword and kill.

In Spoleto, Francis realized that he had been serving himself. He had been his own lord and he had made of himself his master. Francis realized then that he had been living his life in violation of the First Commandment: "You shall worship the Lord your God and him only shall you serve."

In Spoleto, he had begun to understand the primacy of God. That night, he decided to live an upright life and put God first in all of his affairs. Only with God as his foundation could peace begin to take root in his life. His journey to peace began that night when he realized that without God, his life had been aimless, pointless, meaningless.

After he laid down his armor and sword and returned to Assisi, Francis chose the "lesser" way as a penitent. There he would serve a humble, poor, crucified, "minor" God of the Gospels. He took on a life of penance—conversion. Francis' penance consisted in rebuilding churches, fasting, praying, giving away his possessions, living in community, and faithfulness to the Church. His most important moment of conversion, however, was in service to the poor leper.

By serving the leper, Francis learned many things, but especially forgiveness. By placing himself at the feet of the person he despised most, he learned how to forgive. Forgiveness was at the foundation of peace.

Through his encounter with the leper, Francis made a fundamental connection with humanity as he realized that other people, even those he despised most, were not very different from himself. How could he condemn others for their sins while he was fully aware of his own? In his experience with the leper, Francis realized that all people— even the lowliest—have hopes, dreams, aspirations, fears, and pains. That man afflicted with leprosy was someone's child. He was a son, brother, husband, and father; he had once loved and had been needed by others.

Francis realized that all people, including himself, were children of the same Father, which meant that they—from the most beautiful to the ugliest—were his brothers and sisters. Because of his newfound recognition of *his own* sin and suffering, Francis was able to connect with others by relating to and identifying with *their* afflictions. This was Francis' compassion.

Francis found peace by embracing poverty. He had given away his comfortable lifestyle, his right to take over his father's successful cloth business, and his future inheritance. Instead, he donned the penitential tunic and embraced poverty, believing that the Lord would provide him with what he needed. By going down, by emptying himself of all earthly things, Francis allowed himself to be filled with the grace and blessings of the Holy Spirit. After renouncing the ways of the world, Francis sought to remain filled only by the Spirit.

Ultimately, Francis found peace in *minoritas*—lowliness and humility. In order to serve God, he had to change his logic and embrace the logic of God. He had to stop *fighting* people and begin *serving* them in imitation of Christ: "The Son of man came not to be served but to serve" (Mt 20:28). Thus Francis stopped seeking to *increase* his lot in his quest for earthly glories; instead, he sought to go *down* in love toward others.

Francis now had a new Lord he was following: the Christ. The second Person of the Trinity—God almighty, whom "heaven and the highest heaven cannot contain" (1 Kgs 8:27)—had humbled himself by taking on human flesh. He had emptied himself of every heavenly glory because of the greatest love. And the greatest act of love and humility was his death on the cross.

There on Calvary, Jesus identified with and assumed the lowliest part of the human condition: sin. Francis considered the crucifixion the greatest act of divine *minoritas*. And for the rest of his life, Francis sought to imitate Jesus' *minoritas* by embracing humility and the cross. There was his peace and joy.

Essentially, Francis' journey to peace was that of genuine Christianity. By humbly surrendering himself to God, by seeking the will of God, by living a life of penance, by becoming willing to suffer, by forgiving, by serving the poor and seeking justice, by having a humble and surrendered attitude toward personal desires and needs, Francis found peace. The same man who spent his youth seeking worldly desires, entertainment, knighthood, money, and fine clothes discovered peace by leaving everything, serving the poor, and turning his will over to God.

Francis stayed with the Christian crusaders at their camp for several weeks. On August 29, 1219—the feast of the martyrdom of John the Baptist—the crusaders advanced. It was a disaster for them.

They rushed toward the Saracens, who pretended to flee into the desert. But it was a trick, and the majority of the Muslim army, lying in wait, attacked. More than five thousand crusaders were killed that day. If it hadn't been for the command of John of Brienne, along with the fierce resistance of the Hospitallers, Templars, and Alemanni knights, the entire crusader army would have been wiped out.

Francis tended to the wounded and consoled the soldiers. When a truce was called, he seized the opportunity. Francis would go to the sultan. But first, he wanted the permission of the cardinal legate, Pelagius.

However, the cardinal refused Francis' request. "My son, I cannot allow you to go. Surely, they will kill you. We do not need martyrs. We need victory."

The cardinal did not want it to appear that he was sending Francis as an arbitrator. Yet after the persistence of Francis, Pelagius said he could go as long as it was clear that he was not acting on orders of the cardinal.

Armed with nothing but his tunic, cross, and the Word of God, Francis walked together with Brother Illuminato across the battle lines into Saracen territory on a peace mission. Illuminato was from the area of Arce near Rivotorto and had been one of the first to join the fraternity. Neither knew what would happen to them.

Francis was hoping to be able to meet the sultan, Malek al-Kamil, and preach to him and his court. Francis wanted to tell him that, on the cross, Jesus made all people brothers. All were created in the image of the Lord and were redeemed by the blood of Christ. He hoped the sultan would accept his Christian embrace and would, in turn, embrace Christianity. Then the war would stop.

However, Francis was reasonable, and he knew what the other outcome could be: his martyrdom.[1] He knew he could be killed immediately, as there was a Saracen bounty for the head of any Christian. But this did not frighten him. In fact, he hoped for such a great reward for his faithfulness to his Lord.

Francis had been on many peacemaking missions during his life, as his era was marked by considerable conflict: pope versus emperor, Guelph versus Ghibelline, Assisi versus Perugia, Major versus Minor, hierarchy versus heretic, bishop versus mayor, town versus town, family versus family. Through Francis' own experience of peace, he was able to help others find peace—first with God, then with others.

Francis had been successful in negotiating peace many times. Once he had ended a civil war in Siena when he preached a sermon that brought all of them back to peace and unity.[2] Another time, Francis and Sylvester arrived in Arezzo to find the city embroiled in civil war to the extent

---

1 The original thirteenth-century sources all indicate that Francis sought to convert the sultan to Christianity. Various modern interpretations suggest that Francis went to the sultan seeking not to convert him but merely to dialogue. I have presented the meeting according to the traditional account, which I believe is true to the "historical" Francis and not to the modern "spirit" of Francis.

2 See "The Little Flowers of Saint Francis," in *Francis of Assisi: Early Documents*, ed. and trans. Regis J. Armstrong, vol. 3, *The Prophet* (Hyde Park, NY: New City Press, 2001), 11.

that destruction was very close. Francis prayed and the demons fled the city, restoring peace.[3] Just before he died, Francis also helped reconcile warring families in Bologna, as well as in Assisi, when he reconciled the bishop and mayor.

When Francis attempted to negotiate peace, he did not merely seek diplomacy, statecraft, or realpolitik. For him, peace was not something that could be "negotiated" or "made." Nor did Francis merely seek to stop the factions from warring with one another. Francis' attitude toward peace was no different from his attitude toward life: he was a Christian, and his response toward life and its complexities was always Christ.

For Francis, peacemaking flowed from a personal and subjective relationship with the incarnate God in the Person of Jesus Christ. Peacemaking was always built on a concrete and lived experience of the gospel of Jesus Christ.

True peace meant confronting war and hatred with the gospel of Jesus Christ. Only Christ could bring about true peace. Taking away the occasions of conflict could temporarily remove struggle; yet this only led to the *appearance* of peace. For long-term, authentic peace to take hold, the gospel had to be present.

In other words, true peace between individuals or groups in conflict with one another could not be negotiated by merely removing the tension and taking away the possibility of struggle and violence. Instead, the presence

---

3 See Thomas of Celano, "The Remembrance of the Desire of a Soul," in *Francis of Assisi: Early Documents*, ed. and trans. Regis J. Armstrong, vol. 2, *The Founder* (Hyde Park, NY: New City Press, 2000), chap. 74, 108.

of the gospel had to be achieved. In place of violence and conflict, Francis preached love, humility, fraternity, and reconciliation.

With the gospel, there could be forgiveness, respect for the other, fraternal concern, compassion, and care for others. "The work of justice will be peace; the effect of justice, calm and security forever" (cf. Is 32:17).

Francis' model in peacemaking was based on the incarnation of Christ, his coming into the world. Just as the Word became incarnate and came down into the world—in all its ugliness and sin—so did Francis seek to get involved in the complexities and difficulties of the world. He sought to get inside conflict and directly engage the world where the world was—always with and through Christ.

He did not try to bring peace to others as one on the outside. Rather, he had become a brother to all people with whom he fraternally shared his life experience. He did not expect to bring peace into the world by merely withdrawing and praying for the world (which he did periodically). Rather, he was a Christian and kept the gospel of Jesus Christ at the center.

Perhaps most importantly, while seeking to negotiate peace, Francis always believed that peace first had to be personally received before being applied to conflicts. Francis always counseled the friars to carry peace in their hearts.[4] He believed that preaching, teaching, or trying to mediate peace was fruitless unless the peacemaker had peace within.

---

4 See "The Legend of the Three Companions," in *Francis of Assisi: Early Documents*, vol. 2, *The Founder*, chap. 14, 58.

When provoked, Francis possessed within himself the ability to respond with humility and patience instead of reacting with anger or pride. This poor man had renounced everything: money, position, politics, and worldly honors. As he had dispossessed himself of everything, he approached conflicts neutrally, not as one with something to lose or gain.

Ultimately in peacemaking, Francis sought to embrace first and preach second.[5] Though Francis lived in an era of thick walls, fortifications, arms, exclusion, and separation, he always sought to break down walls through an encounter. The encounter Francis had with Christ in the little Church of San Damiano led him to extend that encounter with Christ to others—the Christ he received was the Christ he gave.

His embrace broke down the walls of *physical* leprosy; his embrace broke down the walls of *moral* leprosy; his embrace led to the breakdown of *spiritual* leprosy. In meeting the sultan, Francis hoped to embrace him, and in that embrace, Francis hoped to break down walls and extend Christian fraternity and community to the highest level.

But this would be a very different mission. The people that Francis would now be encountering were not Christian.

---

5 Francis shows his brother friars how to deal with brigands who live near their hermitage in the woods. Francis tells the friars to get the best bread and wine and go out into the woods to serve the brigands. They are to address them as brothers. Then, only after they have eaten to their fill should they talk about the goodness of Christ to them. They are to serve the thieves with humility, good humor, and respect. St. Francis, "The Beginning or the Founding of the Order and the Deeds of Those Lesser Brothers Who Were the First Companions of the Blessed Francis in Religion," in *Francis of Assisi: Early Documents*, vol. 2, *The Founder*, 90.

They had different sacred books, different theology, and
different ideas about the nature of God. They did not understand Christ, the Incarnation, the Gospels, the cross, the
Resurrection, baptism, or the Eucharist.

This was not merely a conflict between European families, clans, or political powers back home, all of whom
were Christians. The Crusade was the "Great War," and
the division between Christianity and Islam was the "Great
Wall." It was a clash between two civilizations and two
worlds. The Christian crusaders considered Islam to be the
Great Evil and the World of Darkness. Nonetheless, Francis had to try.

He walked with Brother Illuminato under the blazing
desert sun with a hot southwest wind blowing from the
Nile. As soon as they were in Saracen territory, Francis saw
Muslim sentries in the distance approaching fast on their
camels. He sensed their desire to harm him and Brother
Illuminato as one of them rode up to him and began whipping him with his riding crop and shouting in a strange language. He felt the sting as he doubled over.

The soldiers threatened decapitation, as the heads of
Christians brought a good bounty. They jeered and laughed
with hatred in their hearts as they bound Francis and Illuminato. Francis knew that hatred well.

The Saracens reminded Francis of a wolf he encountered
in Gubbio some years earlier. Francis had been called to
Gubbio to bring peace to the town, as a fierce wolf was
terrorizing the townspeople, attacking their animals, and
maiming farmers. Terrified and enraged, the citizens
had dispatched numerous armed soldiers and citizens to
kill the beast without success.

Despite the astonishment and objections of the people, Francis set out in the woods to confront the wolf. Francis believed that all creatures of God—whether or not they had rational minds—were created purely in the goodness of God. So Francis preached the gospel to the wolf, saying, "Brother Wolf, I come in peace in the name of Jesus Christ, savior of all."

This disarmed and calmed the wolf. Francis told him that the townspeople were terrified of him because he was so ferocious. Francis then listened to the grievances of the wolf, who said that he attacked the townspeople out of vengeance because they were constantly attacking him with their weapons. Furthermore, he was a wolf and he had to eat; he was hungry.

Francis said that the townspeople, too, were angry with him, since he attacked them and their sheep. Next Francis admonished the wolf for attacking and destroying people and other creatures made in the image of God. Francis then told the wolf about Jesus and the cross.

The wolf slowly acknowledged his own wrongdoing and accepted the mercy and forgiveness of Christ. Then he was able to begin to forgive the transgressions of the townspeople toward him. Francis returned to Gubbio with the wolf and told the people that the wolf desired what any of them wanted: peace, security, food, and affection.

Francis promised that the animal would cause them no more harm as long as they promised to take care of the wolf and forgive in the name of Christ. Francis brought the wolf into the city gates. The people watched in shock as Francis told them that the wolf asked their forgiveness for all the harm he had ever caused them.

The townspeople, in turn, responded with forgiveness, and they prepared the gentle wolf a warm meal. They fed him and cared for him as kindly as one of their own. The wolf lived peacefully within the city walls as a gentle lamb until his death two years later.[6]

As Francis recalled the incident with the wolf, the Saracens continued to whip and beat the friars. Then the two brothers called out the name of the sultan, "Malik Al-Kamil." The Saracen soldiers did not kill the two.

Perhaps Francis had disarmed them by responding to them in a peaceful manner. Or maybe they believed the two had been sent by the crusaders' leader with a message. Or perhaps they believed they wanted to renounce their Christian faith and embrace Islam. For whatever reason, they took the two poor friars to the sultan—the ruler of Egypt.

Sultan Malik al-Kamil had been born in 1180—just one year before Francis. Seven years later, his uncle, Saladin, had led his Muslim army to victory over the Latin Kingdom in the Holy Land, thereby reestablishing Jerusalem under Muslim rule. Saladin's father (al-Kamil's grandfather) had founded the Ayyubid dynasty, and al-Kamil's father ruled over a large part of the Middle East, giving Malik control of Egypt at the young age of twenty.

Sultan Malik al-Kamil was a devoted ruler who built dams, improved irrigation, created schools for the study of Islam, and negotiated trade pacts between cities in Egypt and Italy. He was a man of culture. He often studied

---

6 See "Little Flowers of Saint Francis," chap. 21. It can be considered an allegory for Franciscan peacemaking. However, the bones of an actual wolf are still preserved today in a church near Gubbio. They are believed to be from the same wolf that Francis tamed.

medicine and astronomy and surrounded himself with learned men and doctors.

Religiously, he was a deeply prayerful orthodox Sunni Muslim. He read poetry and had memorized much of the Quran. Al-Kamil had a reputation among Christians for tolerance toward them in Egypt, and he was much more open-minded than previous sultans.

Francis and Brother Illuminato were taken to the sultan's tent. The contrast between the two brothers and the sultan was impressive. The Muslim prince was vested in a silk robe, seated on a throne in a luxurious tent with exotic animals. He was surrounded by a court of clerics, chamberlains, and military captains. In walked two emaciated and beaten friars in tattered habits.

The sultan demanded to know why they were there.[7] "Do you have a message for me, Franks, or do you wish to become Muslims?" Al-Kamil asked. *Frank*, meaning "Frenchman," was the term used by Muslims for crusaders and Christians.

Francis spoke in French, as there were members of the sultan's court who understood the *lingua franca*, the common language. "The Lord give you peace![8] I have not been sent by men but by God Most High."[9]

---

7 No historical record exists documenting what transpired between Francis and the sultan. The following account may or may not have happened.

8 Thomas of Celano said that Francis always began his sermons with those words. "The Life of Saint Francis," in *Francis of Assisi: Early Documents*, ed. and trans. Regis J. Armstrong, vol. 1, *The Saint* (Hyde Park, NY: New City Press, 1999), chap. 10, 23. Francis himself said the same in "The Testament," in *Francis and Clare: The Complete Works*, trans. Regis J. Armstrong (Mahwah, NJ: Paulist Press, 1982), 23.

9 Cf. Bonaventure of Bagnoregio, "The Major Legend of Saint Francis," in *Francis of Assisi: Early Documents*, vol. 2, *The Founder*, chap. 9, 8.

Francis continued, "The mercy of God has made me a brother to all creatures, but especially to all men, since man more than any other creature bears the image of God and has been redeemed by Christ. I did not come to become Muslim but rather to bear the peace of Christ."[10]

At the mention of the name of Christ, murmurs and shouts of blasphemy went up among the sultan's courtiers. The clerics demanded at once that the two infidels be decapitated, which the law required, since they had spoken against their faith.

The sultan realized right away that this Christian Frank before him was not like the others. He was struck by the fact that Francis greeted him and the men of Mohammad not as his enemies but as brothers. He was also impressed by the peace this poor friar exuded from within. This non-threatening poor man did not come with a sword; instead, he came in humility and poverty. He appeared to be holy and he did not seem to be seeking personal gain.

But first the sultan sought to tempt the Frankish pauper. He quieted the protestations of his courtiers and offered Francis wealthy gifts of precious jewels, gold, and silver. But Francis refused, saying, "I seek to imitate the poverty of my poor Lord, Jesus Christ, his holy Mother, and his disciples. I cannot accept wealth."

The sultan already knew the Frank would reject his gifts. He thought to himself how Francis appeared to be practicing *Zakat*, one of the five required pillars of the Muslim faith requiring believers to give away their income and embrace purity.

---

10 Cf. ibid., chap. 9, 4.

The sultan asked him about the peace that appeared to reign in his heart. Francis was never afraid to proclaim the gospel of Christ, but always in a way that was nonviolent, open, and honest.[11] In this, Francis modeled Scripture: "Always be prepared to make a defense to any one who calls you to account for the hope that is in you, yet do it with gentleness and reverence" (1 Pt 3:15).

Francis then preached to the sultan and his courtiers about the origin of his peace and how it came from his abiding faith in Jesus Christ. He said that no one could be saved outside the name of Jesus. When he did so, there were more murmurs and shouts of sacrilege as the courtiers tried to provoke Francis.

Yet Francis never argued with them; instead, he sought to be subject to them, all the while proclaiming Jesus Christ.[12] Francis wished to be "minor" or "lesser" to everyone: priests, nobility, prelates, and even the Saracens. In this, he was like the minor Jesus who meekly embraced his cross without resistance.

The sultan asked Francis why he should become a Christian. He said, "You think of my uncle, Saladin, and I as savages. Yet I ask you, who is more chivalrous? When your Frankish crusaders conquered Jerusalem in 1099,

---

11 Francis wrote—also in the same chapter of the Earlier Rule of 1221—that the friars should "proclaim the word of God when they see that it pleases the Lord."

12 In dealing with nonbelievers, Francis wrote that the friars should "not engage in arguments or disputes [with them], but to be subject to every human creature for God's sake (cf. 1 Pt 2:13) and to acknowledge that they are Christians." St. Francis, "The Earlier Rule," in *Francis and Clare: The Complete Works*, chap. 16.

your brother Christians sacrilegiously carried out mass murder. You slaughtered ten thousand Muslims while they were seeking refuge in our Al-Aqsa Mosque.

"Yet when Saladin took back Jerusalem in 1187 after the defeat of your king at the Battle of Hattin, Saladin graciously allowed Christians to leave the city safely. Further, when your King Richard—the Lion-Hearted you call him—was wounded by Saladin's army, my uncle offered his personal doctor to aid him. For us, this was a 'just war,' and Saladin's actions were out of respect for Jerusalem as a holy city.

"And what did your Christian soldiers do against their own? Just fifteen years ago, you Franks slaughtered your own brother Christians. You Frankish crusaders looted, terrorized, and vandalized your own Christian city of Constantine [Constantinople] for three days while you murdered other Christian Rumi.[13] I ask you again, who is more chivalrous?"

At that moment, Francis heard a strange chanting sound coming from outside the tent. Immediately the sultan and everyone else simultaneously knelt down facing the same direction. They were praying.

Francis would soon discover that the Muslims prayed in such a way five times a day. The way they prayed seemed to him bizarre—the mysterious chanted language, the prayer mats with strange decoration, everyone facing the same direction, bowing and kissing the ground. It was

---

13 *Rumi* was the term used by Muslims for Orthodox Christians, while *Frank* was used for Latin or Catholic Christians. In 1204, Catholic crusaders sacked Constantinople, killing many Orthodox Christians.

quite different from Catholic liturgies, rich in incense and Gregorian chant.

Francis asked the sultan what they said in prayer. Malek al-Kamil responded, "While we pray, we testify before God that there is none worthy of worship but him and that Muhammad (peace be upon him) is his slave and his messenger. We ask God to send his peace and blessings on his messenger Muhammad (peace be upon him) as he did on the Prophet Abraham (peace be upon him)."

The sultan continued, "When we pray, we proclaim that God is the greatest. I bear witness that there is none worthy of worship but God. I bear witness that Muhammad is the prophet of God—come to prayer, come to success, God is the greatest, there is no deity but God. When we finish praying, we Muslims turn our face to the right and the left, offering a greeting of peace to those surrounding us, saying, 'Peace be upon you and the mercy of Allah.'"

Francis stayed with the sultan and his court for several days while they talked. Francis began to realize that the Saracens he was encountering were not like the people he thought they were. He was not encountering uncivilized savages; in reality, the people of the sultan's court were faithful and learned.

Yes, their religion was different and they did not accept the Trinity, the atoning blood of Jesus Christ, or the sacraments. Yet there were elements he could agree with: they were steadfastly devoted to prayer and believed in one God. Francis began to consider that these strangely dressed "Saracens" were brothers to him, not only because they were created by God in his image, but because they, too, believed in and prayed to one God. For Francis, fraternity was now extended to include even people of the Muslim religion.

The sultan, for his part, was content to have discovered a Christian *sufi*, an inner mystic who had encountered the one true God within. We can never know what impressed the sultan the most—Francis' inner peace, his respectful way of interacting with the Muslims, his refusal to give in to wealth and riches, or his way of responding to war with the peace of Jesus Christ.

Perhaps it was the purity of his faith when he challenged the clerics to a trial by fire. Francis, convinced that his religion was true, believed that he would not be harmed while walking across hot coals. Yet, ever practical, he added that if he were indeed harmed, it would not be due to the falsity of his religion, but a result of his own sins. While the clerics turned away, cowering, Francis stood with conviction and resolution.[14]

Yes, the sultan was impressed by this poor Frank who professed Christ. He came in peace unlike the others who brought the sword. Yet the sultan, a devout Muslim, believed that this poor *sufi*—like all the Franks—was in error in believing that Allah could be both one and three at the same time. To the sultan—and all Muslims—Jesus was merely a prophet and did not have a divine nature.

In the end, no conversions took place after the encounter between the poor Francis and the learned al-Kamil.[15]

---

14 Cf. Bonaventure, "Major Legend," chap. 9, 8. This "trial by fire" is enshrined in one of the Giotto frescoes in the upper basilica in Assisi.

15 In "Little Flowers of Saint Francis," chap. 24, the text says that the sultan wished to convert to Christianity, but if he did, his followers would rise up and kill him as well as Francis. Therefore, he asked Francis to send

Nevertheless, something very important happened between the humble Christian friar and the Muslim sultan. Even though the Crusade did not end and peace between the Christians and Saracens did not follow their meeting, something generous, beautiful, and new still took place.

The leader of the Muslim religion of Egypt was moved to respond with a gesture of peace: he turned over the administration and control of the Christian holy sites in Muslim territory to the followers of Francis. In fact, Christian access to the holy sites was one of the reasons the Crusades were launched to begin with.

The sultan also left Francis with gifts, an ivory horn and a prayer mat.[16] Finally, the sultan gave Francis a letter of safe conduct to travel freely and securely throughout the Muslim territories.

Now the Mother Province of the Order of the Holy Land could be established, and Francis was free to walk in the footsteps of his Lord. He promptly went to Palestine, accompanied by a retinue of the sultan's soldiers. When he walked into the Church of the Holy Sepulchre, he wept with great joy.

He stood for a long time in prayer at Calvary where Christ died. A short distance away, he knelt in the tomb where Christ was buried and resurrected. Francis would

---

his friars to baptize him on his deathbed, which they did. This is the first ancient text to indicate that the sultan converted, yet its authenticity is doubtful for the fact that it was written more than one hundred years after Francis died.

16 These two gifts are preserved in the reliquary chapel in the Basilica of St. Francis in Assisi.

never forget the kindness and goodness of his brother, Sultan Malik al-Kamil.[17]

Francis' brother friars have remained in the Holy Land ever since. The majority of Christian churches in Israel—from Judea to Galilee—and the surrounding areas in the Holy Land are still administered by the Franciscan Custody of the Holy Land. The friars still maintain the same three roles they did in the century of Francis: they maintain the sanctuaries, offer hospitality to pilgrims, and serve the local Christian community.

---

17 It is not known whether Francis ever arrived in Jerusalem, mainly because the thirteenth-century sources make no mention of Francis ever going there. The first historian to mention that the sultan provided Francis with a letter of safe passage and that Francis went to Jerusalem was Angelo Clareno, writing one hundred years after Francis died.

16

INCARNATION AND GRECCIO

And while they were there, the time came for her to be delivered. And she gave birth to her first-born son and wrapped him in swaddling cloths, and laid him in a manger, because there was no place for them in the inn.

LUKE 2:6–7

CHRISTMAS was extremely important to Francis, but not in an abstract theological way. He was never a heady academic seeking to grasp the divine mysteries intellectually or theologically. Rather, he sought to live them with his heart, spirit, and emotions.

For Francis, Christmas had to be real. And he celebrated the nativity of the Child Jesus with "immense eagerness above all other solemnities, affirming it was the Feasts of Feasts, when God was made a little child and hung on human breasts. He would kiss the images of the baby's limbs thinking of hunger, and the melting compassion of his heart toward the Child also made him stammer sweet words as babies do."[1]

---

1 Thomas of Celano, "The Remembrance of the Desire of a Soul," in *Francis of Assisi: Early Documents*, ed. and trans. Regis J. Armstrong, vol. 2, *The Founder* (Hyde Park, NY: New City Press, 2000), 151, 199.

In the Incarnation, the nature of God was most obvious to Francis. Christmas recalled the day when the Son of God, born of the Virgin Mary, lay wrapped in swaddling clothes in a manger. In the Incarnation, God revealed more about himself to mankind. Before, he was even more mysterious and hidden, known to a lesser degree: "In many and various ways God spoke of old to our fathers by the prophets" (Heb 1:1). Yet in Jesus, God had become near: "But in these last days he has spoken to us by a Son, whom he appointed the heir of all things, through whom also he created the world" (Heb 1:2).

His coming was foretold from of old: "For to us a child is born, to us a son is given; and the government will be upon his shoulder, and his name will be called 'Wonderful Counselor, Mighty God, Everlasting Father, Prince of Peace'" (Is 9:6).

In the Incarnation, "the goodness and loving kindness of God our Savior appeared" (Ti 3:4). God was revealed as kindness and love. Almighty God humbled himself by coming down from heaven's royal throne (cf. Ws 18:15) and taking on human flesh in the womb of a virgin. God finally appeared and showed himself.

In this event, something new has happened: No longer was God far away, aloof, and remote from humanity up in heaven; now he has appeared and has come into the world. In the Incarnation, we finally know God Face-to-face.

God has appeared as a child born in a stable in Bethlehem, not in the palaces of kings. This is the "epiphany"— the manifestation of God: The human that God becomes is a child, a babe. Now the Almighty God, the Eternal Father is a child—in all his weakness, neediness, and dependence.

In Jesus' humanity, the profound humility of God was revealed. God's nature was shown to the world. The Son of God was born in the poverty of the stable as a child. God—the giver of life, the Creator of creation—became dependent, in his human nature, on human life and love. The Creator became a part of creation. The Incarnation revealed the humility and simplicity in the nature of God.

Francis' spirituality was ever practical, concrete, and tangible, and his faith life involved his entire being. Francis needed to enter into that human-divine mystery by seeking to see, touch, feel, and make present the events of the human life of Christ. He couldn't just think or talk about the life of Christ; he had to live it.

Francis needed to be close to his Savior, to live the gospel fully, and to retrace his footsteps with his mind, body, and spirit. He meditated constantly on the historical life of Christ: Christ's words, his deeds, and important life events—especially the humility of the Incarnation and the charity of the Passion. Thomas of Celano said, "Francis used to recall with regular meditation the words of Christ and recollect his deeds with most attentive perception. Indeed, so thoroughly did the humility of the Incarnation and the charity of the Passion occupy his memory that he scarcely wanted to think of anything else."[2]

So in 1223, just three years before he died, Francis did something entirely new: he sought to make our understanding of the Incarnation come alive by reenacting the nativity

---

2 Thomas of Celano, "The Life of Saint Francis," in *Francis of Assisi: Early Documents*, ed. and trans. Regis J. Armstrong, vol. 1, *The Saint* (Hyde Park, NY: New City Press, 1999), chap. 30, 85.

of Jesus. To our knowledge, this kind of devotion had never been done before.

So it was that Francis was in Greccio, a small village in the Rieti valley near Rome, during the season of Advent. Francis knew and loved the Rieti valley well, as he often passed through Rieti on his journeys to or from Rome. It was like a second home to Francis.

There he prayed often in the four hillside hermitages, and important events in his life took place. In Poggio Bustone, he greeted people with his famous expression, *Buon giorno, buona gente* (Good morning, good people). In Fonte Colombo, he wrote his final Rule approved in 1223. In La Foresta, he sought counsel for his eye disease. The Rieti valley still to this day remains simple and beautiful, unspoiled and pure, the way it was in Francis' era, untouched by mass tourism. Yet it is known mostly for Greccio—the site of the first nativity scene.

Francis came to Greccio for the first time in 1217. There he preached to the townspeople and converted many. One such man was John of Velita. He was a knight, but upon hearing Francis' words, he gave up his life of privileges and nobility to follow Francis in the Third Order. In place of wealth and honors, he chose simplicity and holiness.

John begged Francis not to leave and wanted to build a permanent hermitage in Greccio for him and the friars. Francis agreed on the condition that it be built outside the town. Tradition says that they called a young boy to determine where the hermitage would be built.

John gave the child a bow and a flaming arrow, which he would shoot. Wherever it landed would be the site of the friars' hermitage. The child shot the arrow not a few yards but two miles from Greccio to the top of a cliff near a cave.

Before the beginning of the season of Christmas, Francis called on John to assist him to prepare a life-size nativity scene. He asked him to find a way to demonstrate the inconveniences of the circumstances of the Savior's birth—to show how he was born in a manger with hay and an ox and donkey nearby.[3] Word spread that something new was going to take place. People came from all over the valley and beyond.

A thousand torches illuminated the darkness in a long procession over the fresh snow on the road from Rieti to Greccio. They were friars and clerics, nobility and commoners, and more. They were pilgrims and members of the faithful, in addition to some who were just plain curious.

When Francis finally arrived, his heart was elated as he rejoiced at the crowds. When he looked upon the manger and the animals, his heart melted and he was overjoyed. Simplicity was glorified, poverty was made rich, humility was exalted. The brothers sang, the laity praised God, and even the animals were jubilant.

Bethlehem was in Greccio. In the stable at Bethlehem, Francis could touch and caress the Christ child, like Simeon in the Temple. In everything, there was solemnity, beauty, and joy.

The priest celebrated the Christmas Mass over the manger and all were consoled. Francis himself participated in the Mass vested as a deacon and proclaimed the holy Gospel in chant. Then he preached to all the people about the

---

3 See ibid., chap. 30, 84–86.

birth of the poor King in the poor city of Bethlehem. He preached in a strong, sweet, clear, and sonorous voice. At the elevation of the Host, Francis saw a vision: a little child lying in the manger.

Afterwards, the hay that had been placed in the manger was preserved so that it might be used to restore health. Many of the animals of the surrounding area were freed from various diseases after eating some of the hay. Also, women who had been suffering long and hard labor had an easy delivery after placing some of this hay upon themselves. Finally, an altar was constructed over the manger and a church was built over the grotto.

No one had ever done such a thing before, and this was something quite new. In fact, Christmas had not always been a major feast in the Church. For the early Church, the primary feast was Easter. And this precedence never changed.

Yet through Francis and the experience of Greccio, something new took place: A new emphasis was placed on Jesus' humanity and earthy life. The humility and simplicity of God was revealed with a new profundity. Thus a tradition began each year to recreate the nativity scene of Jesus. In time, it began to be called a crèche, a name that comes from the town of Greccio.

17

STIGMATA AND LAVERNA

I have been crucified with Christ; it is no longer I who live,
but Christ who lives in me.

GALATIANS 2:20

T HE year was 1224. Francis was tired, his youthful vigor gone. He found himself reflecting back on his life rather than looking to the future. Much had happened since the pristine early days with the first brothers at Rivotorto.

In 1212, his first female follower, Clare, had begun religious life. Many convents and women's monasteries all over Europe were switching to her way of life, modeled after the Franciscan way.

In 1215, Francis had attended the Fourth Lateran Council in Rome, where he met Dominic, the founder of that other great mendicant Order of the day.

The following year, Pope Honorius granted the Pardon of Assisi, which allowed anyone who made a pilgrimage to the Portiuncula to receive a plenary indulgence.[1]

---

1 It was remarkable that the plenary indulgence would be attached to the Portiuncula, since there were very few ways to receive the indulgence at that time. One could receive it only by making a pilgrimage to Compostela, Rome, or the Holy Land, or else by fighting in one of the Crusades. In fact, there was resistance to the Portiuncula indulgence among clergy and

The next year, more than five thousand brothers from all over the continent came together there at the Portiuncula for prayer, fellowship, and direction in what was being called the Chapter of Mats. That same year, Francis was able to journey to the Holy Land, where he was successful in negotiating for the friars to take custody of the Christian churches and places of worship there.

In 1221, he responded to the many lay men and women who were seeking to follow him in droves by writing a letter that gave form to the new lay movement. It was called the Third Order.

In 1223, his Rule was finally approved for the Order after a first attempt had been rejected two years earlier.

It seemed clear that the prophecies had been fulfilled: Francis had done great things. In the end, he had become a great spiritual prince. Or had he?

Despite all the accomplishments, Francis was feeling sadness. The truth is that he felt nostalgia for the early years when the brothers were young and few in numbers. That's when he had felt the freest. "The more zeroes, the fewer heroes," he and the first brothers liked to say to one another.

But now things were different, and among the thousands of men who had entered, some were demanding change. Many of them even wanted to change the Rule, in particular, to how it related to poverty.

---

prelates from the other cities who felt it would take away from devotion and pilgrimages there as well as lessen enlistment in the Crusades. This may explain why the Portiuncula indulgence does not appear in any of the earliest biographies, appearing only by the mid-thirteenth century. Perhaps Francis and the early Franciscans, always reluctant to oppose the clergy, would not have wanted to create division and resentment.

There had been too many men for Francis to deal with effectively. His gifts were charismatic, not administrative. In fact, in 1220, Francis had been forced to step down and turn over leadership of the Order to Brother Peter Catani. The following year when Peter died, Brother Elias took the helm, becoming minister general.

After Francis returned from the Holy Land, he realized that the Order had gone in a different direction from what he had originally envisioned. His dream of total poverty—living as itinerant apostles while alternating between prayer and service—had been challenged. The bishops were turning to the friars, asking for help in the Church's struggle against heresy; they were encouraging the friars to settle down for proper study so they could be trained to be effective preachers and confessors.

Within the Order, many of the friars were aging and in need of proper care. In addition, some had entered the Order who did not share Francis' views on poverty. They were seeking privileges and exemptions from different parts of the Rule.

Many were heady intellectuals immersed in the theological debates in the universities. They had never met Francis and did not understand him. Some even considered him a simpleton.

Then, on the other side of the spectrum, a reactionary group of friars had emerged. They lived exclusively in the hillsides and mountain hermitages and clung to radical poverty. Many were influenced by the writings of a Cistercian monk named Joachim of Fiore, who had prophesied a future era of the Spirit that would be led by two poor men. Even though the bishops had criticized his writings, some of these friars believed Joachim's prophecies were being fulfilled in the persons of Francis and Dominic.[2]

Altogether, the Order had become divided into two very distinct camps—each side was acrimonious and jealous of the other. This caused Francis great anguish and sadness.

On top of everything else, Francis' health was failing him, and he was losing his eyesight. When he traveled, he was no longer able to walk, and he rode painfully on the back of a donkey.[3] He was considering that maybe he had been too harsh on his body.

He had always followed the teachings of the Roman Church. But he was wondering whether he had picked up some of the dualistic beliefs of the Cathars after all. Maybe depriving his body of food and sleep, using rocks for pillows, and rolling around naked in thorn bushes and the snow had all been excessive.

---

2 In truth, these friars—called "Spirituals" or "*Fraticelli*"—emerged later in the thirteenth century. They regarded the wealth of the Church as scandalous and were critical of the authority of the hierarchy as well as the leadership of their own Franciscan Order. They were eventually declared heretical in 1296 by Boniface VIII, and the movement died out. Even though they were not historically present during the final years of Francis' life, there was already a movement within the Order clinging to poverty as envisioned by Francis.

3 "The Assisi Compilation," in *Francis of Assisi: Early Documents*, ed. and trans. Regis J. Armstrong, vol. 2, *The Founder* (Hyde Park, NY: New City Press, 2000), 91, said, "When he was traveling through the country preaching and he became sick and could no longer go on foot, he would occasionally ride a donkey, since he did not want to ride on a horse unless compelled by the greatest necessity." See also Thomas of Celano, "The Remembrance of the Desire of a Soul," in *Francis of Assisi: Early Documents*, vol. 2, *The Founder*, chap. 5.

Yes, he wanted to imitate Jesus' passion and the cross; yes, he wanted to discipline the flesh, where sin dwells; yes, he avoided eating meat and large meals in solidarity with the poor. Yet maybe it had all been too harsh. He began asking his body for forgiveness for his excesses.[4]

Francis now admitted that perhaps he had been a little naïve. He had once hoped to truly change the world and make it a better place. He felt that he and the brothers would have been an example to the people, and that a new era of Christian peace would be ushered in because of their way of life. He actually believed that once everyone discovered the beauty of the gospel—of living simply, of giving away what they did not need, of sharing their possessions and time, of serving the less fortunate—they would actually live it.

Francis was once again feeling the sting of that old familiar temptation: to believe that his life had been a failure; that he hadn't amounted to anything; that he hadn't done anything great; that he would never be a prince. It is true that Francis had long ago renounced knighthood and the things of the world, and he had not desired carnal things in a long time. Yet through his Order and movement, he had become a spiritual prince, a knight of the spirit.

The prophecy had been fulfilled. Or had it?

In fact, Francis was forced to admit that he had enjoyed his success. Even though he called himself a great sinner, he sought out humiliations and penances, and he strove to

---

4 "The Legend of the Three Companions," in *Francis of Assisi: Early Documents*, vol. 2, *The Founder*, chap. 5, 14, says, "Because of [excessive fasting], he confessed on his death bed that he had greatly sinned against 'Brother Body.'"

serve the least of society. So he enjoyed the knowledge that he had accomplished something great for the Lord.

Even so, now everything he had accomplished seemed to be ending in failure. Everything was unraveling. Francis felt confused and his doubt returned. He was feeling as if he had failed his namesake, John.

With all this inner anguish and suffering, Francis did what he had learned to do some twenty years earlier in San Damiano. He went to the cross. He was feeling more and more connected to Jesus on the cross. He had spent so much of his life with his gaze fixed on his Beloved who hung on the cross.

Like Peter, Francis had once felt tempted to take Jesus' place on the cross, to take away his pain somehow (cf. Mk 8:27–35). But he understood, as Peter eventually did, that Jesus had to suffer. Christ embraced his passion for the salvation of humanity, but he did so out of love. Francis desired in his heart to stay with Jesus on the cross in suffering, but also to remain connected to the great love that Jesus had for all humanity.

From the beginning of his conversion, Francis never ceased to preach the cross. His relationship with the cross began at the little Church of San Damiano. From the moment he received the locution in the first church he rebuilt, compassion for the Crucified Lord was impressed deep within his soul.

He had carried the wounds of the Lord Jesus and the sacred Passion deep in his heart, though not yet on his flesh. From that time on, his heart had always melted when he thought of the Lord's passion and the cross. He had inflicted his body with such fasting, crying, and abstinence that, whether healthy or sick, he had hardly ever wanted to indulge his body. And the cross that he had received interiorly at San Damiano would soon be miraculously revealed exteriorly on his body.

The cross for Francis was not just an abstract theological idea; it was a way of life. Francis would often say, "But in this we can glory: in our infirmities and bearing daily the holy cross of our Lord Jesus Christ."[5] Francis had learned how to internalize the cross by embracing sufferings and weaknesses.

In doing so, he found contentment, joy, and even strength. He received strength and power in weakness and glory in tribulations and afflictions (cf. 2 Cor 12:9). For Francis, the cross was the foundation of God's love and redemptive mercy.

He knew that surrendering and losing himself for Christ was the way to true life. He understood that his "crosses" were not a sign of God's disfavor but were, rather, a sign of God's glory. He never gloried in anything save in the cross of our Lord.[6]

Francis' favorite story—the one he never tired of telling—was about the cross. One winter day, Francis and Brother Leo were returning to St. Mary of the Angels from Perugia. It was a brutally cold winter, and Brother Leo was suffering greatly. But Francis, smiling, turned to him and said, "Even if one of our brothers gives sight to the blind, heals the paralyzed, drives out devils, gives hearing back to

---

5 St. Francis, "The Admonitions," in *Francis and Clare: The Complete Works*, trans. Regis J. Armstrong (Mahwah, NJ: Paulist Press, 1982), 5.

6 Cf. Celano, "Remembrance," chap. 154, 203.

the deaf, and makes the lame walk, write that perfect joy is not in that."

Then Francis said again in a strong voice, "Brother Leo, if a friar knew all languages and sciences, and if he also knew how to prophesy and to reveal not only the future but also see the secrets of the consciences and minds of others, write down and note carefully that perfect joy is not in that."

Brother Leo, still suffering from the cold, finally asked, "Francis, I beg you in God's name, what is perfect joy?"

Francis responded, "When we come to St. Mary of the Angels, soaked by the rain and frozen by the cold, all soiled with mud and suffering from hunger, and we ring at the gate and the porter comes and says angrily, 'Who are you?' and we say, 'We are two of your brothers,' and he contradicts us and says, 'You are not telling the truth, you are two rascals who deceive people and steal from the poor. Go away!' Oh, Brother Leo, write that is perfect joy! And if we endure all his insults and injuries with patience, oh, Brother Leo, write that is perfect joy!

"And now hear the conclusion, Brother Leo. Above all the graces and gifts of the Holy Spirit that Christ gives to his friends is that of conquering oneself and willingly enduring sufferings, insults, humiliations, and hardships for the love of Christ. For we cannot glory in all those other marvelous gifts of God, as they are not ours but God's, as the Apostle says, 'What do you possess that you have not received? But if you have received it, why are you boasting as if you did not receive it?' (cf. 1 Cor 4:7).

"But we can glory in the cross of tribulations and afflictions, because that is ours, and so the Apostle says: 'May

I never boast except in the cross of our Lord Jesus Christ, through which the world has been crucified to me, and I to the world!'" (cf. Gal 6:14).[7]

With pain in his heart and soul, Francis knew he needed to go on another retreat to a mountain hermitage. Francis had climbed many mountains in his life. But he did not know that he was about to ascend his last one: his Mount Calvary.

Some years earlier, while on a preaching mission through the Marches of Ancona in 1213, Francis had been invited to preach at a banquet hosted by a noble count named Orlando of Chiusi. That evening, the nobleman heard the gospel preached in a way he never had before. Something welled up within him and inspired him to offer Francis part of the mountain towering over Chiusi as a place of prayer and contemplation.

It was called Laverna.[8] Dante would describe it as the "harsh crag" between the Tiber and the Arno.[9] Francis promptly went there with some brothers and found its harsh

---

7 Adapted from "The Little Flowers of Saint Francis," in *Francis of Assisi: Early Documents*, ed. and trans. Regis J. Armstrong, vol. 3, *The Prophet* (Hyde Park, NY: New City Press, 2001), chap. 8.

8 Mount Laverna (also called by its Latin name, Alverna) stands at 3,800 feet above sea level. Francis came here six times in his life; the last time was when he received the stigmata. Today an important spiritual sanctuary here welcomes thousands of people each year on retreat or pilgrimage. It has a large community of O.F.M. friars, including a novitiate and several dormitories for retreatants.

9 See Dante Alighieri, *The Divine Comedy of Dante Alighieri: The Italian Text with a Translation in English Blank Verse and a Commentary by Courtney Langdon*, vol. 3, *Paradiso* (Cambridge: Harvard University Press, 1921), http://oll.libertyfund.org/titles/2311.

nature, biting cold, whipping winds, and twisted, craggy peaks perfect for penance and secluded prayer.

There was a saying among the locals that at the moment of Jesus' death on the cross, the rocks of Laverna had been torn apart and split open.[10] Laverna would be an ideal place for Francis to pray and fast for the Lent of St. Michael the Archangel from the Assumption to Michaelmas.

So Francis and his closest companions—Angelo, Leo, and Masseo—set out on foot from the Portiuncula. They took the Via Antica road toward Perugia. At the town of Collestrada, precisely where Francis and the Assisians had lost the battle to Perugia some twenty years earlier, the poor brothers took the road north along the Tiber River, called the Alta Valle del Tevere (the High Valley of the Tiber).

They continued to the city of the castle (now known as Città di Castello), where they spent the night in a hermitage to the east of the Tiber atop Mount Citerone, called Santa Croce di Nuvole (Holy Cross of the Clouds). After Francis arrived, he exclaimed, "*Oh, che buon riposo!*" (Ah, such rest!). For this reason, the town is known today as Buonriposo.

After a night's rest, the friars continued north past the village of Sansepolcro (Holy Sepulchre). This town had been founded in ancient times upon a stone taken from the Church of the Holy Sepulchre by a crusader returning home; in its cathedral was an ancient image of the *Santo Volto* (Holy Face) of Jesus. Francis continued to the hermitage of Monte Casale, which he had founded earlier in 1212 after serving lepers there. They spent the night there with the brothers.

---

10 According to "Little Flowers of Saint Francis," Second Consideration, this was revealed to Francis.

Francis and the friars then walked northward to the town of Caprese. He admired the majesty of the mountains set behind the town. Francis had no way of knowing that two centuries later a child—named after St. Michael the Archangel—would be born in that village who would spend his youth looking at those same vistas. Michelangelo, son of Lodovico Buonarroti, would follow St. Francis in the Third Order and become one of the greatest artists the world would ever know.

Francis and the brothers crossed the Tiber River at the bridge of Santo Stefano and began climbing up the steep mountain to Chiusi. Finally, after two days on the road, they passed by Count Orlando's castle on the eve of the Assumption. They looked up the steep peak atop Mount Laverna known as La Penna and, realizing that Francis was too weak to make the climb, they borrowed a donkey from a local peasant for Francis to continue. Finally, they ascended the steep switchback and arrived at the hermitage near the top of Mount Laverna.

Once settled at the hermitage, Francis chose to remain isolated from the community so he could pray privately throughout his retreat. He crossed a makeshift bridge over a ravine that led to a hut where he would pray and fast for the next forty days. He told Brother Leo that he wished to be alone and he would eat very little.

Each morning Brother Leo was to come with one loaf of bread, saying, "Domine, labia mea aperies" (O Lord, open my lips). If Francis responded, "Et os meum annuntiabit laudem tuam" (And my lips will sing your praises), Brother Leo was to leave the bread. If not, Francis would not eat that day.

Francis prayed profoundly with his heart over the next forty days. At the end of the fast, Francis knew what his final prayer would be.

Over the past few years, he had become more and more united with God. He had sought more and more to avoid being distracted by worldly things. Despite his sadness for the way things had gone in the Order and in his life, he had generally enjoyed more and more peace.

He was neither excited by mundane desires nor moved by his passions. He kept his mind fixed on God and his attention turned to him. He had perfected charity by practicing virtues, serving others, and loving God habitually.

Since San Damiano, he had kept within himself an intimate desire to be in the presence and fullness of his Beloved on the cross. Now he wished to unite himself with his Beloved with an even greater burning desire. It was like fire.

On the feast of the Exaltation of the Cross, Francis made the prayer of a saint who had dedicated his life to the cross. He asked the Lord for two gifts: to feel in his body the pain that Jesus felt during his passion and to know in his heart the love that Jesus felt for all humanity. This was the two-fold prayer of sacrifice and charity—to feel in his body the pain of the cross, but also in his heart the love that Christ had for all people. The cross, in fact, is the ultimate sacrifice, the ultimate charity of God.

As he made this prayer, a fiery and brilliant six-winged angel appeared.[11] The angel was a Seraph—the angel of

---

11 See Bonaventure of Bagnoregio, "The Major Legend of Saint Francis," in *Francis of Assisi: Early Documents*, vol. 2, *The Founder*, chap. 13.

fire and the highest in the orders of angels. It was rare for the Seraphim—like the Cherubim—to intervene in human affairs. Yet that day, a Seraph did.

When the angel arrived near the saint, there appeared between its wings the resemblance of a crucified man, his hands and feet fastened to a cross. As the angel was disappearing, Francis felt fire in his heart. Immediately, the marks of nails began to appear in his hands and feet just as he had seen a little before in the figure of the man crucified in the angel. As his hands, feet, and side were pierced with the wounds of Christ, Francis felt excruciating pain.

His first biographer described the stigmata in detail: "The marks in his hands and feet consisted of flesh forming on the palms of his hands and tops of his feet as black heads of nails. On the opposite sides, flesh formed as the twisted ends of nails. The side was like a lance wound and it bled for the rest of his life."[12]

Though Francis was doubled over with pain, his soul was rapt with all the ecstasy of joy, love, charity, and sacrifice that could be contained in the heart of a created being. Francis now contained in his heart, soul, and body that connection

---

12 See Thomas of Celano, "The Life of Saint Francis," in *Francis of Assisi: Early Documents*, ed. and trans. Regis J. Armstrong, vol. 1, *The Saint* (Hyde Park, NY: New City Press, 1999), II, chap. 3. There are numerous testimonies to the existence of the stigmata of Francis. All the four early biographies mention it, including Thomas of Celano (here and in his *Second Life*) and Bonaventure in "The Legend of the Three Companions." Additionally, it was referenced by the blessing to Brother Leo by Francis; three surviving letters of Pope Gregory IX (who canonized Francis); Popes Innocent IV and Alexander IV; Jacques de Vitry; Julian of Speyer; Fra Salimbene; Thomas Eccleston; and Brother Elias, who wrote a letter to the entire Order announcing the death of St. Francis.

between true charity and true sacrifice: "Love and truth will meet; / justice and peace will kiss" (Ps 85:11 NABRE).

The life of Francis was now inexplicably and mysteriously united to that of Christ. The incarnation of Christ, the "masterpiece" of God's creation—indeed, the whole purpose of creation (in the future words of the great Franciscan theologian, Blessed John Duns Scotus)—culminated in the Passion and crucifixion as the highest expression of God's love, charity, and mission. The life, love, and mission of Christ marked by the two great feasts of Christmas and Easter were reflected by two events in Francis' life: the reenactment of the nativity scene at Greccio (incarnation) and the reception of the stigmata at Laverna (crucifixion).

Now Francis could say with the Apostle, "I have been crucified with Christ; it is no longer I who live, but Christ who lives in me" (Gal 2:20).

In Laverna, Francis reached the highest and final point of the Christian life: divinization. This is a stage that only the great saints reach in this world, but all saints reach it in the next. The Word became flesh not only to take away sin in atonement for the rupture with God caused by Adam but also to give to man the divine life and to make us partakers of the divine nature. As St. Athanasius had said, the Son of God became man so that we might become like God.

Francis had spent twenty years seeking to imitate Christ and be transformed *spiritually*. There on Laverna, Francis was transformed *physically* through the crucifixion marks of Jesus. He became like the God in whom he believed. He was fully divinized. He became like God.[13]

---

13 For more on the theological concept of divinization (*theosis* in Greek), see *Catechism of the Catholic Church*: 460, 1988.

Francis had now passed through all three stages of the spiritual life: the *Via Purgativa* (the Purgative Way), in which he sought to convert his will to the will of God through his penance; the *Via Illuminitiva* (the Illuminative Way), in which he sought to learn more about God and draw closer to him; and now the *Via Unitiva* (the Unitive Way). Francis was fully united to God. He was a "channel" of God's grace and love. He was fully love.

After receiving the holy and terrible wounds, he was filled with awe toward God. The following words flooded his heart. He wrote them on a parchment and gave them to his beloved companion, Brother Leo:

> You are holy, Lord, the only God, You make wonders.
> You are strong, You are great, You are the most high,
> You are omnipotent, Holy Father, King of heaven and earth.
> You are Three and One, Lord God of gods;
> You are goodness, all good, the highest good, Lord, God,
>   living and true.
> You are love and charity; You are wisdom;
> You are humility; You are patience;
> You are beauty; You are security; You are calm;
> You are joy and levity; You are our hope;
> You are justice; You are temperance,
> You are everything, our riches, enough for us.
> You are beauty, You are meekness;
> You are our protector, You are our guardian and defender;
> You are strength; You are refreshment.
> You are our hope, You are our faith,
> You are our charity, You are all our sweetness,
> You are our eternal life: Great and wonderful Lord,
> God almighty, Merciful Savior.[14]

---

14 Translation by the author. The original parchment is conserved in the reliquary chapel within the Basilica of St. Francis.

Francis described his Creator in beautiful words. These words expressed not only who God was to Francis but also what Francis became as a result of his walk with him—his divinization. However, they also describe what all who believe in him can become as a result of each person's own walk with the Lord. We, too, can become like God; we, too, will become God.

In Laverna, the cross showed Francis the truth about his life. He was in good company. The truth is that Jesus' earthy life, too, finished in apparent failure. Jesus Christ—whose kingdom was not of this world—ended his worldly life up there on the cross, while most of his followers had fled. It seemed that Jesus' own heavenly Father had abandoned him.

Jesus may also have been tempted to believe that he had accomplished nothing as he hung on the cross. Not only was Jesus not the worldly messiah the Jews hoped for who would usher in a powerful political movement to counter the Roman occupation; it appeared that even his kingdom of heaven on earth had failed, too.

In Laverna, Francis finally understood what every great visionary and founder of every religious movement eventually realizes: that the Order Francis had founded was not really his; that he had never really been in control of it to begin with; that he had been given a mission to accomplish not for himself but for Someone else; that everything he was given must eventually be given back to the One who gave it; that before the Lord, Francis was what he was and nothing more. The Lord gives, and the Lord takes away (cf. Jb 1:21). Everything was God's—the Order, his health, his accomplishments, the brothers—everything.

The truth is that the spiritual life is not something we can acquire, conquer, or achieve. We can never do enough penances, make enough pilgrimages, fast enough, pray enough, serve enough, humiliate ourselves enough. No, the spiritual life cannot be earned. It does not come through achievements or successes, nor is it lost in failure. It comes through fidelity and surrender.

Francis was forced to accept that this world, though created good and redeemed in Christ, was not his final destination. All the goodness, joy, and blessings he and the brothers had experienced and received in this world—which they, in turn, had shown to others—were merely a foretaste of the eternal life to come. This world, though good, was still broken and would not change until Christ himself came once again.

Francis had indeed been successful and faithful to his namesake, John. He was not a failure. He had lived his mission well—he was a herald of the Lord.

Despite his sadness, weaknesses, and failures, Francis now had true peace. Despite his apparent failures in this world—both worldly and spiritual—the stigmata were the visible seal stamped into his flesh by God himself as a sign of his approval of Francis and his life. God was, indeed, pleased with Francis, whose life was simply to follow the cross. The greatest and most accomplished thing Francis could have ever done was to have faith in Christ and to show the way to him.

Francis never spoke of what he experienced on the mountain. In fact, he ordered those brothers who witnessed the marks not to tell anyone as long as he remained alive.[15] With renewed peace in his heart, Francis left the mountain of Laverna and returned to Assisi. His new all-encompassing love for all people and the world consumed him. Yet it did not keep death from approaching and overtaking his flesh.

---

15 See Celano, "Remembrance," chaps. 98–101.

18

TRANSITUS

I glorified you on earth by accomplishing the work that you gave me to do. Now glorify me, Father, with you, with the glory that I had with you before the world began.

JOHN 17:4–5 NABRE

W HEN the brothers were staying in Foligno, Brother Elias had a dream. An elderly priest clothed in white appeared to him and said, "Get up, brother, and tell Brother Francis that eighteen years have passed since he renounced the world and clung to Christ. He will remain in this life only two more years; then he will go the way of all flesh when the Lord calls him to himself."[1]

Francis spent the last two years of his life in great pain and suffering from his ailments, though he never complained. After receiving the imprint of the cross on his body on Mount Laverna, he was summoned to the Rieti valley, where he met Cardinal Hugolino, Bishop of Ostia and guardian of the Franciscan Order. Hugolino had always

---

1 Thomas of Celano, "The Life of Saint Francis," in *Francis of Assisi: Early Documents*, ed. and trans. Regis J. Armstrong, vol. 1, *The Saint* (Hyde Park, NY: New City Press, 1999), chap. 8, 109.

had a filial affection for Francis, and he suffered greatly for Francis' physical conditions.

There in Rieti, the cardinal encouraged him to receive treatment to try to regain his eyesight. It was risky, as the practice of medicine was primitive. Doctors performed crude surgeries while barbers carried out the ancient practice of bloodletting. Most sick people trusted more in the intercession of the saints than the hands of doctors.

Yet Francis agreed to the procedure, although it frightened his brothers. The doctor cauterized Francis' head in several places, opened his veins, put on plasters, and applied eye salves. But it was of no help, and his eye condition worsened. Before leaving Rieti, Francis predicted that the cardinal would one day become the Bishop of Rome. Indeed, on March 19, 1227, he was elected pope, taking the name Gregory IX.

Francis returned to Assisi and stayed for some time in a hut next to the Church of San Damiano. There he had received his call some years earlier to rebuild the Church, and Clare and her sisters were now living there in a monastery. Racked with pain and suffering, he was cared for by the sisters while he prayed to God for strength to be able to bear the pain.

The agony did not go away, but Francis did receive the grace he asked for. Instead of giving in to his suffering, Francis wrote a prayer blessing the Creator for his creation and the elements. Though he could barely see, he closed his eyes and recalled, in brotherly and fraternal affection, the sun, moon, stars, wind, water, fire, and earth—a prayer now known as *The Canticle of the Creatures*.[2]

---

2 This prayer/poem remains to this day one of the most beautiful works of early Italian literature.

Francis then went to a hermitage in Siena, where he finally began to succumb to the evil that was overtaking him. His stomach was racked with illness and his liver was infected, causing him to vomit blood. He may have had tuberculosis or, as some suspect, even leprosy.

Brother Elias heard what was happening and came quickly to be with him. Together they went to a hermitage outside the city gates of Cortona known as the Cells. There, Francis' abdomen began to swell along with his legs and feet. His stomach ailment grew worse and he could hardly eat.

Francis now understood that he was dying, and he asked to be taken back to Assisi. Despite his illnesses and encroaching death, Francis still said to the brothers, "Let us begin again to serve the Lord God, for up to now we have made little or no progress."[3]

For some time now, though he could no longer practice penances as he did when he was young because of his illnesses, Francis used to say this, and it frequently surprised the brothers. For Francis was always reflecting on how he could serve God anew. He never believed he had reached his goal, and he untiringly pursued his desire to wholly attain newness of life—even at the end of his life.

It was autumn and the days were shorter. The cold rainy season had begun early that year, and the fragrance of smoke from the wood-burning stoves filled the cool air. Already a sheet of gray fog was blanketing the Umbrian valley. The leaves, changing colors, were dying and falling to the ground, foreshadowing the bitter Umbrian winter that was soon to set in.

---

3 Celano, "Life of Saint Francis," II, chap. 6, 103.

Francis was taken to the residence of the Bishop of Assisi, where he stayed for several days. There he felt inspired to add the final lines to his *The Canticle of the Creatures*: "Be praised, my Lord, through our Sister Bodily Death, from whose embrace no living person can escape. Woe to those who die in mortal sin! Happy those she finds doing your most holy will. The second death can do no harm to them."

Francis now understood that death was no longer his enemy; it was merely part of the journey—the *Transitus*. He requested that when his time should come, Brother Angelo and Brother Leo sing to him the praises of Sister Death.

His last desire was to return to the place he loved more than any other—St. Mary of the Angels, the Portiuncula—the church he believed to be endowed with special graces and blessings. There in the place where he had embraced poverty some twenty years earlier, he would give back to God the last thing he possessed in this world: his life. Several knights carried Francis on a litter from Assisi down to St. Mary of the Angels. When they arrived at the hospital of San Salvatore on the plain halfway between Assisi and St. Mary's, he asked the bearers to stop and place the litter on the ground.

Francis turned and faced Assisi. Though he was by now completely blind, he raised himself up a little and blessed his beloved Assisi, saying, "Lord, just as in an earlier time, this ancient city was, I believe, an abode of wicked and evil men, now I realize that, because of your abundant mercy, and in your own time, you have singularly shown an abundance of your mercies to it. For, 'where sin increases, grace abounds all the more' (cf. Rm 5:20).

"Solely on account of your goodness, you have chosen it for yourself, so that it may become the place and abode of those who know you, in truth, acknowledge you, give glory to your name, strive to live a holy life, of truest doctrine, of good reputation, and of evangelical perfection to the whole Christian people.

"I ask you, therefore, Lord Jesus Christ, Father of mercies, not to consider our ingratitude. Be mindful of your most abundant piety which you have showed to it, that it always be an abode for who truly acknowledge you, and glorify your blessed and most glorious name for ever and ever. Please bless this city and all those who will come here. Amen."[4]

Francis lay down again and was carried the short distance to St. Mary of the Angels.

It was Saturday, October 3, 1226. Francis was forty-four years old. A true minor to his last day, his final desire was to be stripped and laid naked on the bare ground next to the church of the Portiuncula. "You are dust, and to dust you shall return" (Gn 3:19). He wished to return to that fertile Umbrian soil that had produced so many saints before him and from which he himself had come.

He called his brothers together, consoled them, and exhorted them to love God. He told the brothers never to leave the Portiuncula: "See to it, my sons, that you never abandon this place. If you are driven out from one side, go

---

4 These were Francis' words adapted from St. Francis, "A Mirror of the Perfection, *Rule*, Profession, Life, and True Calling of a Lesser Brother," in *Francis of Assisi: Early Documents*, ed. and trans. Regis J. Armstrong, vol. 3, *The Prophet* (Hyde Park, NY: New City Press, 2001), 124.

back in from the other, for this is truly a holy place and the dwelling place of God."[5]

Francis then spoke to the friars with fatherly affection and consoled them over his death. He told them to remain faithful to poverty and to the Roman Church, and he gave the gospel preeminence over any other Rule of Life. He then asked Brother Leo to read him the Gospel of John beginning with the words "Before the feast of the Passover, when Jesus knew that his hour had come to depart out of this world to the Father" (Jn 13:1).

As Angelo and Leo quietly sang his praises to Sister Death, Francis then uttered his final admonition: "I have done what is mine; may Christ teach you what is yours!"[6]

As Francis closed his eyes, he thought he faintly heard the trumpeting of the Assisi city hymn in the distance announcing the end of the day and the closing of the city's gates. He started to feel a deep, profound peace within. He felt the quiet, calm, familiar beckoning of the Holy Spirit—the same voice he had heard numerous times in his life that had said, "You will become a great knight. . . . Whom do you serve? . . . Go and rebuild my house." This time, the voice was calling him for the final time, saying, "Come home, Francis."

---

5 Celano, "Life of Saint Francis," II, chap. 7, 106. In fact, the friars still maintain a community at St. Mary of the Angels. Today it is considered the mother church of the O.F.M. branch of the Order.

6 The end of Francis' life is taken from Thomas of Celano, "The Remembrance of the Desire of a Soul," in *Francis of Assisi: Early Documents*, ed. and trans. Regis J. Armstrong, vol. 2, *The Founder* (Hyde Park, NY: New City Press, 2000), chap. 162, 214, as well as from Bonaventure of Bagnoregio, "The Major Legend of Saint Francis," in *Francis of Assisi: Early Documents*, vol. 2, *The Founder*, chap. 14, 4.

As the sun disappeared behind the hills beyond Perugia in the west, the light in Francis went out. It was now night-time on the fourth day of October. His earthly pilgrimage was finished, though his heavenly one had just begun.

A great flock of larks began circling and singing over-head with unusual joy, strange in that they usually pre-ferred the light of day and avoided the night. The angels and saints in heaven rejoiced: "Precious in the sight of the LORD / is the death of his saints" (Ps 116:15).

On July 16, 1228, less than two years after Francis' death, Hugolino, now Pope Gregory IX—Francis' close friend and protector of the Order—declared in Assisi what everyone already knew: Francis was a saint in heaven.

Now the prophecy was fulfilled. Francis had become a great prince and had done great things. Yet the greatest thing Francis had accomplished was that he had shown the way of the Lord. In this, he had been true to his namesake, John, after all. He was a true herald of the Lord.

The next day, the pontiff personally placed the first stone of the basilica to be built in his honor.[7] *The cross—death—did not have the final word. The Resurrection did.*

---

7 After Francis died, his body was placed in the Church of San Giorgio (today the Basilica of St. Clare). Construction of his new basilica was led by Brother Elias, and had as its goal a beautiful basilica worthy of the most popular saint of the era, in addition to being a place of welcome to the many pilgrims that would come. The site had been called the "Hill of Hell" because criminals were executed there; however, it became known as the "Hill of Paradise" after the church was completed and Francis' remains placed within. Today the church is composed of three levels. The lower basilica was completed after just two years of construction in Romanesque architectural style, and Francis' body was buried deep underneath the main altar. It was designed to be a tomblike burial place. The upper church was

Maybe Francis had never been destined to be a Minor after all. Perhaps he had really been a Major all along. Even though he strove throughout his converted life to embrace lowliness—going down in this world—perhaps the true direction he had been going all along was up. With the angels and saints. Glorified. In heaven. With God. For all eternity. Forever.

---

completed in Gothic style in 1253. The ceilings were higher and its nave brighter to symbolize the Resurrection. The best artists of the day—Giotto, Cimabue, Martini, and Lorenzetti—were called in to embellish both levels. In 1818, excavation was begun to uncover Francis' tomb. After fifty-two days of digging, the sarcophagus was discovered beneath heavy blocks of travertine rock. The space around it was excavated and left austere and simple, true to the spirit of Francis. This created a third level—that of the tomb.

THE CANTICLE OF THE CREATURES

written by St. Francis in 1224 in San Damiano

Most high, omnipotent, good Lord!
Yours are praises, glory, honor, and every blessing.

To You, alone, Most High, do they belong,
And no mortal is worthy to pronounce Your name.

Be praised, my Lord, through all Your creatures,
Especially, my lord, Brother Sun,
who brings the day; and You give light through him.
And he is beautiful and radiant with great splendor.
To You, Most High, he bears likeness.

Be praised, my Lord, through Sister Moon and the stars;
in the heavens You formed them bright and precious and
    beautiful.

Be praised, my Lord, through Brothers Wind and Air,
whether stormy or serene, and all the weather
through which You give sustenance to Your creatures.

Be praised, my Lord, through Sister Water
who is very useful, and humble, and precious, and chaste.

Be praised, my Lord, through Brother Fire,
through whom You illuminate the night;
and he is beautiful, cheerful, robust and strong.

Be praised, my Lord, through our sister Mother Earth,
who sustains and governs us,
and produces various fruits with colored flowers and herbs.

Be praised, my Lord, through those who forgive for love of You;
and endure sickness and trial.

Happy those who endure it in peace,
for by You, Most High, they shall be crowned.

Be praised, my Lord, through our sister Bodily Death,
from whose embrace no living person can escape.
Woe to those who die in mortal sin!
Happy those she finds [doing] Your most holy will
As the second death will do [them] no harm.

Praise and bless my Lord, and give [him] thanks,
and serve him with great humility.[8]

---

8 Translated by the author.

ABOUT THE AUTHOR

Bret Thoman, OFS, has been a member of the Secular Franciscan Order (Third Order of St. Francis) since 2003. He has a master's degree in Italian from Middlebury College, a BA from the University of Georgia in foreign languages, and a certificate in Franciscan Studies. Bret has written and published four books and translated twelve books from Italian to English.

While working as an interpreter for CNN, he translated the papal conclave and announced the election of Pope Francis live. He is also a former commercial pilot and has logged over 3,500 hours of flight time.

Bret's main activity is organizing pilgrimages for St. Francis Pilgrimages, the company he started in 2004. He leads pilgrims throughout Italy, the Holy Land, and along the walking Camminos from Assisi to Rome.

Bret is partial to Latin, Gregorian chant. and incense, and he spends his free time reading, hiking, or visiting new places. He currently lives in Loreto, Italy, with his wife and three children.

INDEX

 TAN·BOOKS

TAN Books is the Publisher You Can Trust With Your Faith.

TAN Books was founded in 1967 to preserve the spiritual, intellectual, and liturgical traditions of the Catholic Church. At a critical moment in history TAN kept alive the great classics of the Faith and drew many to the Church. In 2008 TAN was acquired by Saint Benedict Press. Today TAN continues to teach and defend the Faith to a new generation of readers.

TAN publishes more than 600 booklets, Bibles, and books. Popular subject areas include theology and doctrine, prayer and the supernatural, history, biography, and the lives of the saints. TAN's line of educational and homeschooling resources is featured at TANHomeschool.com.

TAN publishes under several imprints, including TAN, Neumann Press, ACS Books, and the Confraternity of the Precious Blood. Sister imprints include Saint Benedict Press, Catholic Courses, and Catholic Scripture Study.

For more information about TAN,
or to request a free catalog, visit
TANBooks.com

Or call us toll-free at
(800) 437-5876

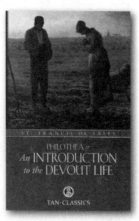
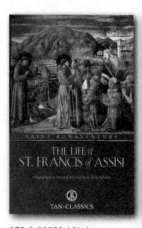

SAINT IGNATIUS OF LOYOLA

The SPIRITUAL EXERCISES *of* SAINT IGNATIUS *at* MANRESA

TAN·CLASSICS

978-0-89555-153-5

ST. CATHERINE OF SIENA

THE DIALOGUE *of* ST. CATHERINE OF SIENA

A conversation with God echoing your spiritual life to the fullest

TAN·CLASSICS

978-0-89555-149-8

EDITED *by* WILLIAM EDMUND FAHEY

The FOUNDATIONS *of* WESTERN MONASTICISM

The Life of Saint Antony of the Desert, The Holy Rule of Saint Benedict, and The Twelve Degrees of Humility and Pride

TAN·CLASSICS

978-0-89555-199-3

The collection includes distinguished spiritual works of the saints, philosophical treatises and famous biographies.

JEAN PIERRE DE CAUSSADE

ABANDONMENT *to* DIVINE PROVIDENCE

TAN·CLASSICS

978-0-89555-226-6

DOM LORENZO SCUPOLI

The SPIRITUAL COMBAT *and* A TREATISE ON PEACE OF SOUL

TAN·CLASSICS

978-0-89555-152-8

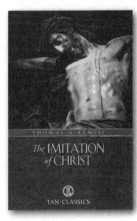

THOMAS A KEMPIS

The IMITATION *of* CHRIST

TAN·CLASSICS

978-0-89555-225-9

Visit us at TANBooks.com

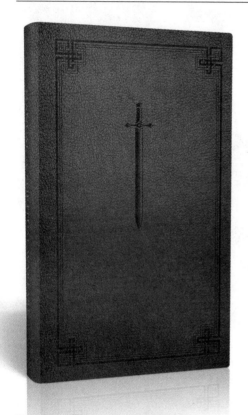

Confraternity *of the* Precious Blood

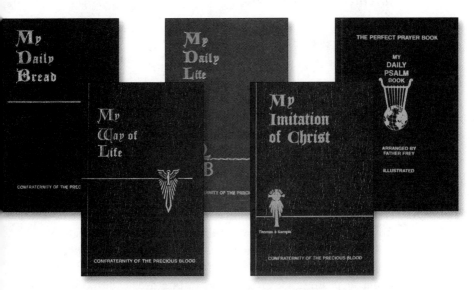

Five little books that make a BIG difference in your spiritual life!

My Daily Bread   Fr. Anthony J. Paone, S.J.

This pocket-sized, daily devotional will strengthen your love for Christ and his teachings and lead you through the three ways of the spiritual life: Purification, Imitation, and Union.
978-1-61890-812-4 • *Pocket Edition*

My Way of Life
Walter Farrell, O.P., S.T.M. &
Martin Healy, S.T.D.
Presents small, concise portions of Saint Thomas Aquinas's *Summa Theologica* in a manageable format.
978-1-61890-833-9 • *Pocket Edition*

My Daily Life
Fr. Anthony J. Paone, S.J.
The follow-up title to *My Daily Bread*. Provides practical advice on daily living. overflows with common sense, compassion, and holiness.
978-1-61890-818-6 • *Pocket Edition*

My Imitation of Christ
Thomas a Kempis
Countless saints from Therese of Liseux to Ignatius of Loyola have used this book to direct their minds during adoration. Ideal for the busy Catholic.
978-1-61890-824-7 • *Pocket Edition*

My Daily Psalm Book
Arranged by Fr. Frey
The powerful prayers of Psalms are presented in compact size to take out and read in spare moments of reflection through the day.
978-1-61890-821-6 • *Pocket Edition*

Spread the Faith with . . .

TAN·BOOKS

A Division of Saint Benedict Press, LLC

TAN books are powerful tools for evangelization. They lift the mind to God and change lives. Millions of readers have found in TAN books and booklets an effective way to teach and defend the Faith, soften hearts, and grow in prayer and holiness of life.

Throughout history the faithful have distributed Catholic literature and sacramentals to save souls. St. Francis de Sales passed out his own pamphlets to win back those who had abandoned the Faith. Countless others have distributed the Miraculous Medal to prompt conversions and inspire deeper devotion to God. Our customers use TAN books in that same spirit.

If you have been helped by this or another TAN title, share it with others. Become a TAN Missionary and share our life changing books and booklets with your family, friends and community. We'll help by providing special discounts for books and booklets purchased in quantity for purposes of evangelization. Write or call us for additional details.

TAN Books
Attn: TAN Missionaries Department
PO Box 410487
Charlotte, NC 28241

Toll-free (800) 437-5876
missionaries@TANBooks.com